Bags

ANNA ALICIA

For Calder

Bags

ANNA ALICIA

SEW 18 STYLISH BAGS
FOR EVERY OCCASION

Photography by
Anna Batchelor

Hardie Grant

QUADRILLE

Contents

Introduction

Bags are my absolute favourite things to make
– for me, they tick all the boxes!

As a freelance craft writer for magazines I get to make all sorts of things, from pillowcases to placemats, but bags are hands-down my first choice. Every bag in this book can be sewn at your kitchen table (they were, in fact, all sewn at mine). You can make a bag in as little as an hour – like the gorgeously simple Fold-over Clutch on pages 64–67. Or you can lavish crafting love on something more involved, like the Boxy Hand-luggage on pages 96–101. Bags are so darn useful and they make the best gifts (including for men – see the Fold-over Backpack on pages 40–47)!

Alongside all this, they offer a fantastic way to develop your sewing skills. If you're new to sewing you can start with something simple, like the Basic Tote on pages 16–19, and build up gradually as you gain confidence. Similarly, if you're already good friends with your sewing machine I hope this book will offer both basic projects to which you can add your own twist, as well as some more involved bags that explore shape and structure, like the Interview Bag on pages 54–59, with its nifty internal divide.

I have to confess I'm a fairly impatient maker, so I've tried to design projects that feel rewarding to make, but where you can see your progress quickly and clearly. I've kept processes as simple as possible and focused on what's necessary and useful – and of course beautiful! The projects explore some ever-so-useful techniques – like squaring corners to create depth or sewing zips – which, as a self-taught crafter, used to fill me with fear until I realized they're really rather simple once you know how.

I hope you'll have as much fun making these bags as I did, and even more fun putting them to good use! There's a particular joy to using handmade things in your everyday life (especially when you did the making!), whether it's bundling your shopping into a tote at the supermarket or rocking the perfect clutch on a night out - enjoy!

How to use this book

Each project comes with detailed but clear written instructions, often with the addition of diagrams or detail photos to help you check everything is looking as it should.

In many of the projects I've noted when it might be useful to take a look at one of the techniques detailed in the Core Techniques section pages 116–131. Here you can find detailed step-by-step photos for some basic techniques that feature across different projects (things like sewing zips or making handles) in case you're not familiar with these or you need a bit of a reminder. I'd also suggest referring to the images of the finished project as you progress, just to check you're on the right track.

All the cut lists and templates include seam allowances, so there's no need to add this when cutting out.

The instructions assume you will remove your pins as you sew – this is how I like to work, but if you have your own way (some people place their pins at a right angle to the stitch line, sew over them and then remove them at the end), then go ahead and work in whichever way you're most comfortable.

It's always a good idea to backstitch a little at the beginning and end of any length of sewing (this just means sewing the first few stitches, then sewing backwards over the those stitches

before sewing forwards again and continuing your sewing, then the same at the other end). This is just to secure your stitches.

FABRIC

It's the beautiful fabrics that really make these bags work. In the materials lists I've given the type of fabrics that work best for each project (some need heavier fabrics like canvas and some work better in lighter ones such as quilting-weight cotton), but from there it's up to you! Also see page 135 for more tips on choosing the right fabrics.

In the materials list I've rounded fabric amounts up to the nearest ¼m (or ⅛yd) that you'll need, so you can easily see how much to buy (especially if ordering fabrics online where you usually order in ¼m or ⅛yd increments). If you're using fabric you already have, you can check the cut lists to see exactly how much fabric you'll actually need.

If I've listed ¼m of fabric this should be a 'fat quarter' – this means the piece has been cut roughly as a square (usually about 50 x 55cm in metric or 18 x 22in in imperial, depending on the width of the fabric), rather than a long strip. Most online fabric suppliers cut in this way – but I have been caught out before, so always check when buying if it will be cut as a fat quarter or a long quarter. Usually online suppliers will state this in the fabric's description details.

CUT LISTS

Most of the projects start with a 'cut list' that details the pieces you'll need to cut from each of your fabrics. I've listed these with height and width next to the measurements – this is particularly helpful if you are using a patterned fabric, because you'll need to think about which way the pattern will end up.

QUICK MAKES

Some of the projects in this book are marked out as Quick Makes – this means they'll probably take you under an hour to make (though there's no need to rush!), which is nice to know if your precious crafting time is limited!

SKILL LEVELS

The skill levels are intended as a guide to help you gauge how involved a project is. If you're new to sewing you might want to start with the projects marked 'easy' and work your way up. The Core Techniques section is here to help you develop your skills and teach you everything you need to know to move on up through the more advanced projects as you feel ready!

●○○ Easy
●●○ Medium
●●● Advanced

ILLUSTRATION KEY

—o —o —o Pin here

- - - - - - - - - - Sew here

.... Continues

⋀⋀⋀⋀⋀⋀⋀⋀ Zip

→ → → → Cut here

Tools and equipment

BASIC SEWING KIT

Sewing machine: This doesn't need to be anything fancy, all you'll need for these projects are straight stitch and zigzag stitch.

Zipper foot: This probably came with your machine, but it can be bought separately if not.

Hand-sewing needle: Though the vast majority of the work here will be done on your machine, there are a few projects where a little hand sewing is needed.

Pins: My favourites are the long pearl-headed type as they are easy to see and remove as you sew. It's a good idea to have plenty of pins, ideally in a little pincushion for easy access.

Safety pins: You'll just need two of these for the projects that involve drawstring cords (see Drawstrings step 2 on page 121) as they offer a nifty way to make threading cords super easy. I always keep two in my pincushion for this purpose!

Tailor's chalk: This is for marking out your rectangles and patterns on your fabric. It comes in several colours – I find it useful to have a white chalk and also a stronger colour in case I'm working on very pale fabric where white won't be clearly visible.

Good-quality dressmaking scissors: You don't need to spend loads here but it's definitely worth investing in a proper pair of dressmaking scissors to ensure your cutting out is both accurate and easy. Keep these exclusively for cutting fabric so the blades don't get blunt.

Basic scissors: These are a must so that you're not tempted to cut out paper patterns with your dressmaking scissors!

Seam ripper: It's a tiny tool but invaluable when things don't go quite to plan and you need to undo some stitching with as little fuss as possible.

Bradawl: This little tool often comes in handy, particularly when using hardware such as Chicago screws (see the Interview Bag project on pages 54–59) or eyelets (see the Pompom Bucket Bag project on pages 72–77), or basically any time you need to poke a hole in your fabric.

Ruler: A wooden ruler works well with fabric, because it doesn't slip.

Tape measure: I can still clearly hear the CDT teacher at school repeating his mantra 'Measure twice, cut once', and I have to admit, he had a point!

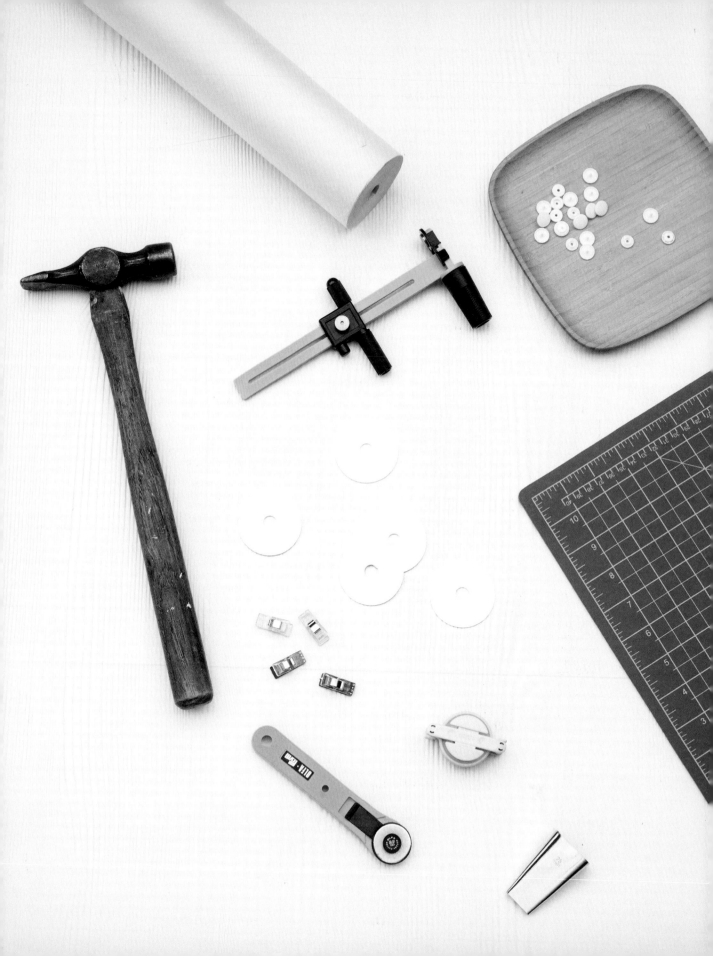

Setsquare: As many of these projects are made up of squares or rectangles of fabric it's really important that your right angles are, well, right! Even if you just have a very basic small plastic setsquare, that'll do the trick.

Iron: Again, this doesn't need to be anything fancy, just your standard iron, but check your settings are appropriate for the fabrics you're using each time you use it.

Tracing paper: To trace out the templates printed in this book.

Cotton machine-sewing threads: It's really good to have a stash of these in a range of core colours including white, cream, black, navy, grey and dark beige, plus the colours you're most drawn to in your fabric choices (in my case, mustard, peach, bright red and mint). This way you can usually find something close enough to your fabric to work.

USEFUL EXTRAS

Rotary cutter and cutting mat: A rotary cutter and cutting mat can save a lot of time if you're cutting out lots of pieces, for instance cutting strips to make bias binding.

Rotary compass circle cutter: This is useful but not essential for the Day-to-evening Bag project on pages 60–63 and gives you a much smoother curved cut than you can achieve with scissors.

Large sheets of plain newsprint paper: For many of these projects you'll need to measure out several rectangles the same size (for instance for front and back, plus lining), so I often find it saves time to draw out the rectangle on a large sheet of paper and use this as a template. This is also really useful if you want to make a bag more than once.

Pattern weights: I often end up weighing down my pattern pieces with random objects that happen to be handy, but for the more organized crafter pattern weights are a useful extra. You can even make your own by sewing little pouches and filling them with rice.

Fabric clips: These are a useful alternative to pins for fabrics that pins would mark, such as paper fabric, or if you're using thick fabrics that can be hard to pin through.

Hammer: This is only needed for adding the eyelets to the Pompom Bucket Bag project on pages 72–77.

Pompom maker, 4.5cm (1¾in) version: You only need this for the Pompom Bucket Bag project (though pompom making can be addictive!).

Bias binding maker, 2.5cm (1in) version: Making your own bias binding is an optional extra on a couple of the projects featured here. Ready-made bias binding comes in a limited range of colours and patterns, and although there are some lovely options out there, making your own gives you the freedom to make exactly the binding you want.

Snap setting tool: This offers a really easy and quick way to add the type of snap fasteners that fix through the fabric, with a cap on the outside that comes in a great range of colours. You can use one of these for the Fold-over Backpack project on pages 40–47. The tool often comes in a kit with the snaps, but sew-on poppers are always a simple alternative.

All these projects are designed to be doable at a small kitchen table.

Everyday

Basic Tote

For me, there's no bag more useful than a tote – from books to trainers to shopping, there always seems to be something that won't fit in my handbag and demands its own tote!

QUICK MAKE

Skill level ●○○

Materials

½m (⅝yd) patterned quilting-weight cotton fabric

½m (⅝yd) plain quilting-weight cotton fabric for lining

3m (3⅜yd) webbing, 2.5cm (1in) wide

Thread to match your fabric and webbing

Basic sewing kit

Cut out

MAIN FABRIC

Two pieces: 42cm (16½in) high x 32cm (12½in) wide

Optional pocket: 42cm (16½in) high x 15cm (6in) wide

LINING FABRIC

Two pieces: 42cm (16½in) high x 32cm (12½in) wide

WEBBING

Two lengths: 130cm (51in)

FABRIC NOTE

Most non-stretch fabrics would work for this simple pattern, from quilting cotton for a light, easily-folded-away tote, to denim or canvas for something more hard wearing.

1   Lay out one of your outer pieces right side up, in a portrait position. Measure 7.5cm (3in) in from the right-hand (long) side and mark a line in tailor's chalk from top to bottom, then do the same on the left-hand side. Take one of your pieces of webbing and, starting from the bottom edge of your fabric, lay the webbing on top so that its outer edge runs along one of the lines you marked, pinning in place. At the top edge, curve your webbing round into a handle (make sure it isn't twisted) and lay the rest of it so that its outer edge lines up with the other chalk line and its cut end is parallel to the bottom edge, pinning in place.

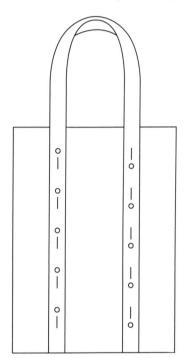

2   Starting at the bottom, sew along one edge of your webbing, about 2mm (⅟₁₆in) in from the edge. Stop 3cm (1¼in) before the top edge of your fabric (where the handle is), sew across the webbing at this point and back down its other edge. Do the same on the other length of pinned webbing.

3   Repeat step 1 for the other outer piece and length of webbing. If you're adding the optional pocket, follow the instructions below marked 'Optional'. If you're not adding the pocket, repeat step 2.

OPTIONAL

To add a front pocket, take your pocket piece and fold it in half, right side out, so that the shorter edges meet. Press the fold. Line up the raw (not folded) shorter edges with the bottom of your outer bag piece and tuck the sides under the webbing, re-pinning as needed to hold it in place. Now repeat step 2, sewing the webbing in place and securing your pocket at the same time.

4   Lay out both of your outer pieces again, right side up. Fold the straps back over the fabric and pin to keep them out of the way.

5   Lay a lining piece (right side down if it has a right side) on top of each outer piece, lining up the edges.

6   Pin and then sew along the top edge only of each of your pairs with a 1cm (⅜in) seam allowance.

7   Unfold along the seam line and press the pieces open.

8   Lay one of your opened-out outer/lining pairs out, right side up, and lay the other right side down on top so that the outers are together and so are the lining pieces.

9   Pin all the way around the edges, then sew with 1cm (⅜in) seam allowance, leaving a 6cm (2⅜in) gap on one of the lining's edges.

DESIGN NOTE

This is a basic pattern, perfect for beginners and ideal for tweaking as you get more confident! For a more roomy tote, you could square off the corners (see Squaring Corners on pages 124–125) before you turn your pieces right side out, giving your tote more depth, or you could add an internal pocket to the lining, or a popper closure...

10 Trim across each of the corners diagonally within the seam allowance and close to the stitching to reduce bulk.

11 Turn your bag right side out through the gap you left. Sew up the gap by machine (it'll be hidden inside the bag) or by hand for a neater finish.

12 Tuck your lining down into your outer – and don't forget to remove the pins holding the handles down.

13 Pin and sew around the top edge of the bag about 3mm (⅛in) in from the edge to hold the layers together.

Shopper Bag

Handmade items that add a little joy to the everyday are my favourites, and these reusable shopping bags do just that! To keep these bags light enough to stash at the bottom of your handbag I've used French seams to create a finished look (even on the inside) without adding a lining.

Skill level ●●○

Materials

½m (⅝yd) fabric

2m (2¼yd) bias binding
(or make your own following the instructions on pages 118–119)

Thread to match your bias binding and fabric

Basic sewing kit

Cut out

MAIN FABRIC

Trace or photocopy **Templates A**, **B** and **C** (see page 133), then cut out.

_____

FABRIC NOTE

A plain or a pattern that works either way up is best for this project, rather than a pattern that has an obvious single direction, as your fabric is folded over to form the front and back.

_____

1   Fold your fabric in half with wrong sides together so the shorter edges meet, and lay out with the folded edge across the top. Draw a 51.5cm (20¼in) high x 42cm (16½in) wide rectangle with a shorter side along the folded edge. Pin the two layers of fabric together and cut out your rectangle along three sides, but don't cut the folded edge.

2   Place **Template A** so the straight side is centred on the folded edge and draw around it.

3   Place **Templates B** and **C** so their corners align with the top corners of the rectangle and draw around them.

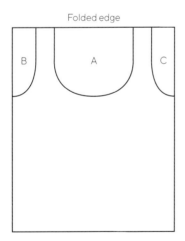

Folded edge

4   Cut out and discard the curved pieces of patterns **A**, **B** and **C**.

5   Pin and sew along your straight sides and the bottom edge with a 5mm (¼in) seam allowance – but don't sew along any of the curved edges. Trim your seams to 3mm (⅛in).

6   Turn your bag inside out and iron well along the seams. Now pin and sew along all the same straight edges again, with a 5mm (¼in) seam allowance.

7   Flatten out the bottom corners of your bag so the side seams lay over the bottom seam and mark a line across 4.5cm (1¾in) from the corner of the seam – see Squaring Corners on pages 124–125 for more information. Sew along the line and then trim the corner seams to 5mm (¼in) and oversew with a zigzag stitch.

8   Turn your bag right side out.

9   Fold your bias binding in half, right side out, (so the long edges meet) and iron to crease. Pin bias binding along each of the curved edges on your bag, so the raw edges of your bag are sandwiched inside the folded binding. Where the ends of your binding meet, overlap by 2cm (¾in), then fold the top layer of binding under by 1cm (⅜in).

10   Sew your binding in place about 2mm (1⁄16in) from the edge.

11   Fold the sides of your bag in so that they are level with the outer edges of your handles to create the boxy shape, and press to crease.

iPad Case

Keep your technology cosy and looking gorgeous with some simple quilting and an easy-to-make case – with optional fancy piping!

Skill level ●●○

Materials

½m (⅝yd) patterned quilting-weight cotton fabric

½m (⅝yd) light wadding (batting)

½m (⅝yd) plain quilting-weight cotton fabric for the lining

35cm (14in) zip for larger version or 25cm (10in) zip for smaller version

1m (1⅛yd) piping in a contrasting colour to your outer fabric (optional)

Thread to match your fabric

Setsquare

Basic sewing kit

Cut out

For iPad Pro

MAIN FABRIC

Two pieces: 30cm (12in) high x 38cm (15in) wide

WADDING (BATTING)

Two pieces: 30cm (12in) high x 38cm (15in) wide

LINING FABRIC

Two pieces: 27.5cm (10¾in) high x 36cm (14¼in) wide

For iPad Mini

MAIN FABRIC

Two pieces: 22cm (8¾in) high x 29cm (11½in) wide

WADDING (BATTING)

Two pieces: 22cm (8¾in) high x 29cm (11½in) wide

LINING FABRIC

Two pieces: 19.5cm (7¾in) high x 27cm (10⅝in) wide

FABRIC NOTE

If you need your case to offer more than basic protection from the odd bump you can add extra layers of wadding (batting) or use a thicker foam interfacing.

1   Lay out your two wadding (batting) rectangles in a landscape position, and place one of your main fabric rectangles on top of each, right side up. Add a few pins to hold the layers together.

2   Using your tailor's chalk and a setsquare, mark a diagonal line across one of your rectangles at a 45-degree angle. Continue drawing lines parallel to the first at 1.5cm (⅝in) intervals all the way across your rectangle. Repeat on your other rectangle.

3   Sew along your lines. Ideally you should use a walking foot on your machine for this if you happen to have one (this is a foot specifically used for quilting). They're a bit pricey so don't feel you should rush out and buy one just for this project – with a regular foot you will just find that the layers shift a bit as you sew and you'll probably end up with some wadding (batting) sticking out. To allow for this I've made the rectangles a bit bigger than you'll need, so you can trim them once you've finished quilting.

4   Trim your rectangles to 27.5cm (10¾in) wide x 36cm (14¼in) high for the larger version, or 19.5cm (7¾in) wide x 27cm (10⅝in) high for the smaller one.

OPTIONAL

To add piping, lay one of your rectangles out right side up in the landscape position and pin your piping around the inside edges of the right-hand short side, bottom long side and left-hand short side. You want the 'tube' part of your piping to be facing inwards and to be 1cm (⅜in) from the edge of the fabric – see Piping on page 123 for more information. Your piping will need to curve neatly around the corners and be flattened down (it'll want to stick up a bit as it bunches up at the corners) – it's worth taking a moment to get this neat. Sew your piping in place 5mm (¼in) from the 'tube' part.

5   Lay out one of your lining pieces right side up. Place your zip on top, right side up, so that its edge lines up with a long edge of your lining. Lay one of your quilted pieces on top, right side down, lining up all the edges – see Inserting Zips on pages 126–127 for more information. (If you're using piping, make sure the non-piped edge is on top of the zip.)

6   Pin along the top edge about 3mm (⅛in) from the zip's teeth.

7   Using a zipper foot on your machine, sew along the edge you've pinned, about 3mm (⅛in) from where you can feel the zip's teeth.

8   Unfold your pieces of fabric and fold back the other way so they are wrong sides together, with your zip sticking out of the seam.

9   Lay your other lining piece out right side up and place your zip on top again, right side up, with its unsewn edge lining up with the long edge of your lining. Place your other quilted piece on top, right side down, pin and sew as before.

10 Open out and re-fold this side, as you did with the other side, so that your fabrics are all right side out. Press along the seams.

11 Pin and then sew about 2mm (1/16in) from the seam on each side of the zip (don't forget to change your machine's foot back to an ordinary sewing foot) to keep your fabrics neatly away from the zip teeth. (If using piping, fold it out before you sew, then fold it flat again.)

12 Fold your fabrics so that the two quilted pieces are right sides together, as are the two lining pieces.

13 Unzip your zip!

14 Pin all the way around the edges, 1cm (3/8in) in. Make sure the zip's teeth are pointing towards the lining side (I always start by pinning where the ends of the zip are to get them pointing the right way).

15 Sew all the way around the edge, but leaving a 6cm (2⅜in) gap on the lining side. (If using piping, be careful to sew close to but not over your piping 'tube' when sewing the outer/ wadding side.)

16 Turn your case right way out through the gap. Sew up the gap (it'll be hidden inside so you can do this with your machine or by hand).

17 Tuck the lining back through the zip and give your case a press to finish.

DESIGN NOTE

Piping can seem a little fiddly, but it creates a really professional, finished look. It's also a great way to add a pop of neon or metallic to a simple design like this one.

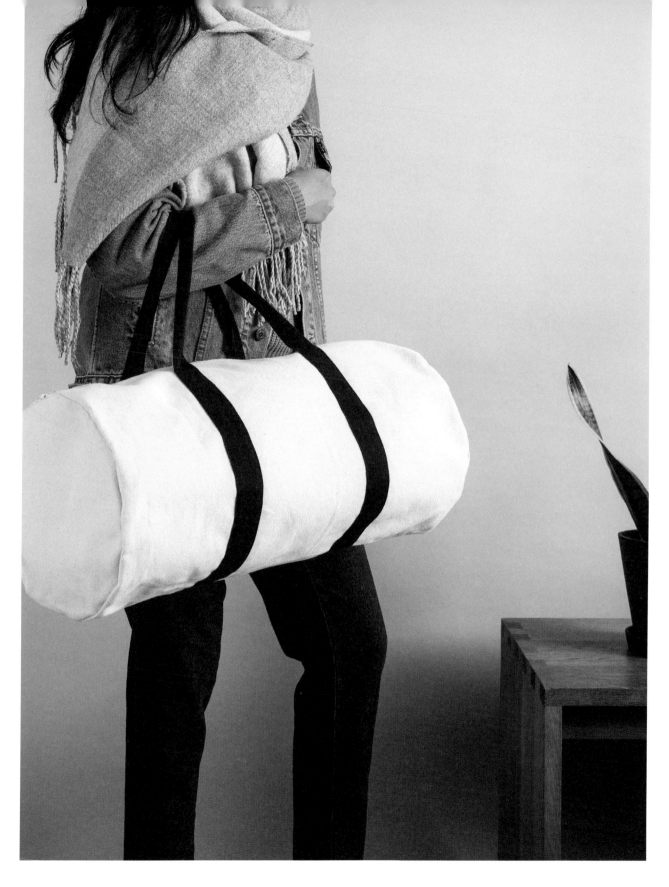

Basic Big Duffel

Pared down to its basic form, this big duffel is a no-frills make. It'll soon be ready to put to work, hauling anything from gym kit to overnight gear.

Skill level ●●○

Materials

1m (1⅛yd) heavy-weight canvas fabric

2½m (2¾yd) webbing, 4cm (1½in) wide (contrasting colour to your canvas)

1½m (1¾yd) webbing, 2.5cm (1in) wide (similar colour to your canvas)

55cm (22in) chunky zip

Thread to match your fabric and outer webbing

Basic sewing kit

Cut out

CANVAS FABRIC

One piece: 84cm (33in) high x 57cm (22½in) wide for body

Two circles: 28cm (11in) diameter for ends

NARROWER WEBBING

Two lengths: 57cm (22½in)

FABRIC NOTE

You need something sturdy, like a heavy canvas, for this project as it's unlined and without interfacing – so all its shape comes from the main fabric. Canvas comes in different weights, so make sure you buy canvas listed as 'heavy'.

---

1   Lay out your canvas (right side up if it has a right side) in a portrait position. Mark a line 16.5cm (6½in) in from each of the longer sides. Next, measure and mark the mid-point along one of your lines.

2   Starting from that mid-point, pin your wider webbing along the inside of your line. When you reach the edge of your canvas allow a 39cm (15½in) loop of webbing, to form a handle, before continuing to pin your webbing along the inside of the other line you marked. Again, when you reach the other edge, leave a 39cm (15½in) loop as a handle, then continue to pin as before until you meet the point where you started. Here, overlap the end of your webbing by 3cm (1¼in) and cut away any excess. Fold your overlapping end under by 1.5cm (⅝in) – so it still overlaps the other end by 1.5cm (⅝in) – and pin in place.

3   Starting at the point where each side of a handle crosses the edge of your canvas, measure and mark 8cm (3⅛in) from the edge on each length of webbing. Starting in the middle, sew along one edge of your webbing strip about 2mm (¹⁄₁₆in) in from the edge until you reach the first mark. Swivel to sew across the webbing, then sew down the second side and across the other end at the mark in the same way, then back to where you started. Repeat on the other strip of webbing.

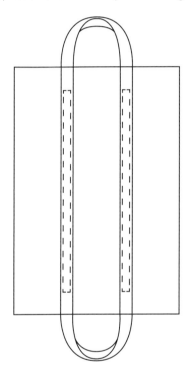

4   To make your handles extra secure, sew a square with a cross in the centre below each of the 8cm (3⅛in) marks – see Securing Straps/Handles on page 128 for more information.

5   Pin your handles back out of the way so they are not overlapping the edges.

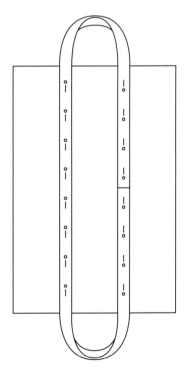

DESIGN NOTE

I pared this bag right back to its basic form – just the cylinder-shaped body, long zip and contrasting handles – but there are loads of ways you could change it up: add a long cross-body strap from end to end, add pockets on the sides or ends…

6   Lay out your canvas again, right side up in a portrait position. Lay your zip right side down on top, so one edge is aligned along one of the shorter edges of the canvas. Lay one of your narrower webbing strips on top of the zip, lining the edge up with the edges of the canvas and zip. Pin along this edge about 5mm (¼in) from your zip's teeth.

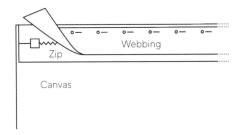

7   With a zipper foot on your sewing machine, sew along the edge you pinned, about 5mm (¼in) from the zip's teeth (normally I'd sew closer, but with the heavy canvas I find it's best to leave a little extra room for the zip's teeth).

8   Rotate the canvas so that the other shorter edge is in front of you. Line up the other edge of the zip to this edge of the canvas, right side down as before (fold the webbing back out of the way). Add your other strip of narrow webbing on top and pin and sew as before.

9   Open the zip. Fold back the webbing on either side of the zip and pin about 1cm (⅜in) from the zip's teeth. Change your foot back to an ordinary sewing foot. Sew along both sides where you've pinned, so that your raw edges end up sealed beneath webbing on both sides of the zip.

10   Leave your zip unzipped.

11   Pin a circle of canvas, right side in, at each end of the fabric 'tube' you've made. Your pins should be about 1cm (⅜in) in from the edge, but I always find it takes a bit of fiddling and re-pinning to get the circles to sit just right. Sew the circles in place where you pinned.

12   Trim the seams to about 5mm (¼in) and then zigzag stitch over the raw edges to stop them fraying (unraveling).

13   Turn your bag right side out through the zip.

14   Finally, you just need to finish your handles. Starting 16cm (6¼in) up from where one of the handles leaves the bag, fold the webbing in half, so the long edges meet, and pin, stopping 16cm (6¼in) from the other end of the handle – see Webbing Straps/Handles on page 129 for more information. Sew about 2mm (¹⁄₁₆in) in along the pinned edge. Repeat on the other handle.

Circle Shoulder Bag

In rebellion against the many rectangles and sharp corners in this book, this bag is all about the curves. I think it's also one of the most versatile bags – ideal for everyday but smart/cute/cool enough for going out, too.

Skill level ●●●

Materials

½m (⅝yd) cotton twill (or similar medium-weight canvas or denim) fabric

¼m (⅜yd) quilting-weight cotton for lining

¼m (⅜yd) stiff fusible interfacing

20cm (8in) bias binding, 2.5cm (1in) wide

20cm (8in) double-sided fusible interfacing tape, 2.5cm (1in) wide (or a thin strip of double-sided fusible interfacing)

30cm (12in) zip

Thread to match your fabrics

Basic sewing kit

Cut out

MAIN FABRIC

Two pieces: **Template A** (see page 132) for front and back

One piece: **Template B** (see page 132) for pocket

Three pieces: 6cm (2⅜in) high x 32cm (12½in) wide for base and either side of zip

One piece: 6cm (2⅜in) high x 110cm (43¼in) wide for strap

Two pieces: 10cm (4in) high x 7cm (2¾in) wide for zip tabs

LINING FABRIC

Two pieces: **Template A** for front and back

One piece: 6cm (2⅜in) high x 32cm (12½in) wide for base

INTERFACING

Two pieces: **Template A** for front and back

One piece: 6cm (2⅜in) high x 32cm (12½in) wide for base

FABRIC NOTE

Even though this is a small bag, a fabric with a bit of body is needed here to hold the circle's curves in place.

1 Start by adding your bias binding to the straight edge of your pocket piece. Place the pocket piece right side up. Open out one of the folded sides of your binding, then with right side down line that edge up along the straight edge of your pocket. Pin and then sew along the crease where you unfolded the bias binding. Lay your interfacing tape along the back of your binding (don't unfold the other edge), then re-fold your binding along the crease you sewed. Fold the binding over the straight edge of your pocket and iron in place to fuse and seal the binding in place.

2 Lay out one of your circles of main fabric right side up and lay your pocket piece on top, also right side up, so the curved edges match up. Pin and then sew around the curved edge of the pocket with a 5mm (¼in) seam allowance. This is now the front panel of your bag. Set aside for now.

3 We'll also prepare the strap, ready for later. Take your long strap piece and lay it out right side down. Fold in half so the long edges meet and press the fold. Unfold and then fold the long edges in so they meet along the crease, pressing again. Fold again along the original crease and pin to keep it folded. Sew along both long sides about 2mm (¹⁄₁₆in) in from the edge – see Making Fabric Straps/Handles on pages 130–131 for more information. Set aside for now.

4 Next we'll prepare the zip. Place one of your zip tab pieces right side down, and fold

both the narrower edges over by 1cm (⅜in), pressing to crease. Then fold the tab in half so the folded edges meet and press again. Repeat with the other tab.

5 Take one of your zip tabs and sandwich one end of your zip tape between its two layers (like the tab is biting the zip!), pin in place. Do the same at the other end of your zip. Sew across the zip tabs about 3mm (⅛in) from where they meet the zip teeth.

6 Take two of your 6 x 32cm (2⅜ x 12½in) strips of main fabric and fold each in half so the long edges meet, right side out, pressing to crease the fold. With the zip right side up, pin one strip along each side with the fold about 3mm (⅛in) from the zip's teeth. Sew each side about 2mm (¹⁄₁₆in) from the folded edge.

7 Trim your zip/fabric panel so that it is 6cm (2⅜in) wide and 30cm (12in) long, making sure you keep the zip in the centre and the tabs at each end an equal size.

8 Place your third 6 x 32cm (2⅜ x 12½in) piece (this is your base piece) right side down and fold over both of the shorter edges by 2cm (¾in), pressing to crease.

9 Lay out your zip panel right side up, and line up one end of your strap centred on top of the tab, so that the rest of the strap runs along your zip. With your base piece right side up, lay the folded edge overlapping the end of your strap/zip panel by 1cm (⅜in) and pin. Sew close to the folded edge of your base piece twice to secure the strap.

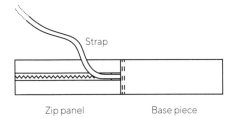

Strap

Zip panel   Base piece

10 Making sure your strap is not twisted, repeat step 9 at the other end of your zip panel so you end up with a circle made up of your zip panel and base piece, with your strap attached at the seams.

11 Turn the zip/base circle wrong side out and unzip the zip. Make sure the strap is tucked inside the circle.

12 Lay out the front panel (prepared in step 2) so it's right side up. Place your zip/base circle on top, making sure that the side seams line up roughly the same distance below the edge of the pocket on both left and right sides, and the zip is centred above the pocket.

13 Pin your zip/base circle to your front panel about 1cm (⅜in) in (I find that in spite of my best measurements this sometimes needs a bit of fiddling to get it to fit exactly!). Sew all the way around with a roughly 1cm (⅜in) seam allowance.

14 Lay out your other main fabric circle piece right side up and pin and sew to the other edge of the zip/base circle in the same way. Leave the bag with wrong sides out.

15 To make your lining, start by ironing your interfacing onto the wrong side of each corresponding piece of your lining (see page 122 for more information on interfacing).

16 Next, fold the narrow edges of your lining base over to the wrong side by 1cm (⅜in) and press. Lay out one of your lining circles right side up, and pin one of the long edges of your lining base, right side down, along one edge of your circle, about 1cm (⅜in) in. Sew along the pinned edge with a 1cm (⅜in) seam allowance. Lay out your other lining circle right side up, and pin the other long edge of the lining base to that circle, sewing with a 1cm (⅜in) seam allowance.

17 Turn your lining right side out and tuck your main bag down inside it (we'll turn everything right side out later!). Line up the folded edges of your lining's base strip so they are roughly the same distance below the ends of the zip on both sides.

18 Fold the curved edges of your lining in by 1cm (⅜in) and pin so they line up with the seams of your outer bag.

19 Hand sew along all edges of your lining – using small stitches and being careful not to sew all the way through your outer fabric, so your stitches won't be visible on the outside.

20 Turn your bag right side out through the zip and zip up!

DESIGN NOTE

The bias binding trim on the front pocket, in a lovely 'watercolour' fabric, is a small touch but it really makes this bag. For the perfect bias binding, follow the instructions on pages 118–119 to make your own.

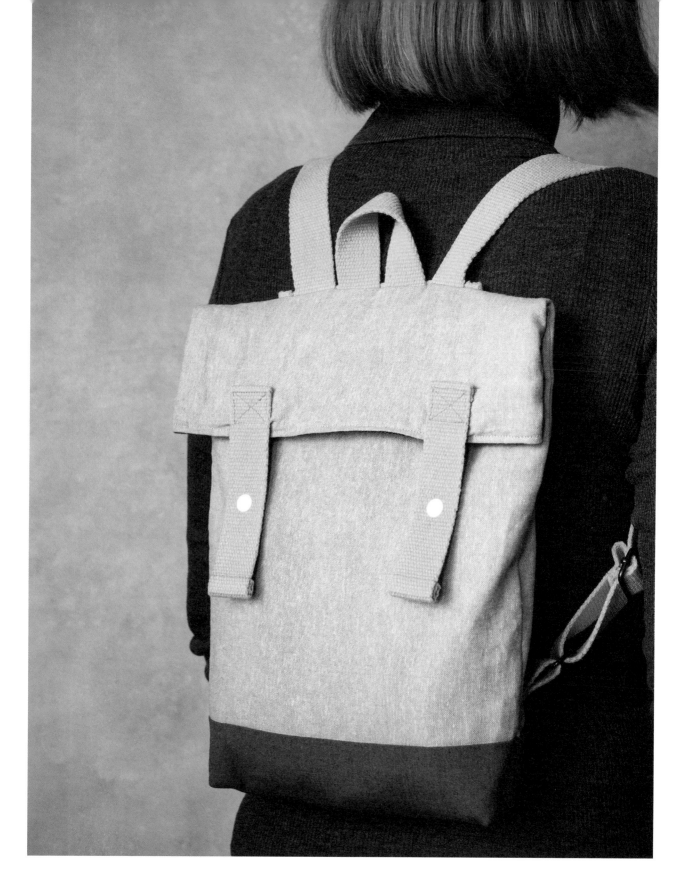

Fold-over Backpack

This is my perfect everyday bag – a comfortable, easy-to-wear backpack style that's a little bit smarter and more compact than most backpacks. I've kept this one simple, but you could add internal pockets to the lining or a front pocket to keep things organized!

Skill level ●●○

Materials

½m (⅝yd) medium-weight cotton, canvas or denim fabric

¼m (⅜yd) medium-weight cotton, canvas or denim contrast fabric

½m (⅝yd) heavy-weight canvas or denim lining fabric

2½m (2¾yd) webbing, 3cm (1¼in) wide

2 D-rings, 3cm (1¼in) wide

2 sliding bar strap adjusters, 3cm (1¼in) wide

2 sets of snap fasteners with fixing tool

You can get these in a kit, but if you don't want to buy a snap fastener tool you could just use sew-in snap fasteners or hook-and-loop tape instead.

Thread to match your main fabric and webbing

Bradawl

Basic sewing kit

Cut out

MAIN FABRIC

Two pieces: 47cm (18½in) high x 30cm (12in) wide

CONTRAST FABRIC

Two pieces: 10cm (4in) high x 30cm (12in) wide for base

LINING FABRIC

Two pieces: 47cm (18½in) high x 30cm (12in) wide

WEBBING

Two pieces: 12cm (4¾in) long for loops

Two pieces: 18cm (7in) long for closure tabs

One piece: 18cm (7in) long for hook loop

One piece: 14.5cm (5¾in) long for hook loop

Two pieces: 75cm (29½in) long for straps

Using medium-weight fabrics for the outer and heavy-weight fabric for the lining gives this bag its structured shape and slightly utilitarian feel.

1   Lay out one of your main fabric pieces right side up, in a portrait position. Measure 8cm (3⅛in) up from the bottom short edge and use your tailor's chalk to mark a line all the way across. Lay one of your base pieces right side down on top, above the line, so its bottom long edge lines up with your chalk line. Pin along that edge and then sew 1cm (⅜in) up from that edge. Fold the base piece down so the unsewn long edge meets the bottom edge of your main piece and press along the seam. This is the front panel of your backpack.

2   With your other main piece, begin in the same way by drawing out your chalk line 8cm (3⅛in) up. This time before we add the base piece we need to add our webbing loops and D-rings for the straps. Thread each loop strip of webbing through one of your D-rings, folding the webbing in half over the straight edge of the D-ring. Place these webbing loops 5cm (2in) in from each long side of your main fabric piece, with their raw ends 7cm (2¾in) from the bottom edge – they should be overlapping the chalk line by 1cm (⅜in) – and pin. Zigzag stitch over the raw ends of your loops to hold them in place.

3   Lay, pin and sew your base piece, then fold it over and press, as you did in step 1.

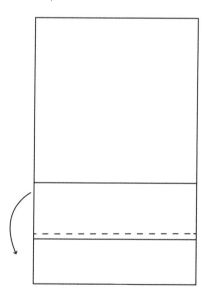

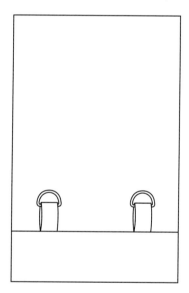

4 Next we'll add the closure tabs to the same panel (although this is the back panel of the bag, when the top is folded over the tabs will be on the front). On each closure tab strip of webbing turn one end over by 1cm (⅜in) twice, pin and sew about 5mm (¼in) from the end. Turn the other end of each strip over by 1cm (⅜in) and pin to your bag panel 5.5cm (2¼in) from the top edge and 6cm (2⅜in) in from each side. Sew a square with a cross from corner to corner at the end you pinned in place – see Securing Straps/Handles on page 128 for more information.

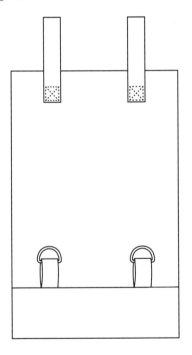

5 Still working on the same panel, we now want to add the hook loop and straps. Take the 18cm (7in) strip and pin in place with its top edge 11cm (4⅜in) from the top edge of your bag panel and centred on both sides. Fold both raw ends of this strip under by 1cm (⅜in) and pin. Fold the 14.5cm (5¾in) strip into a loop and tuck the ends about 1cm (⅜in) under the middle of the strip you just pinned in place.

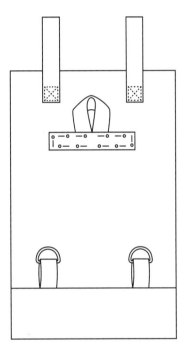

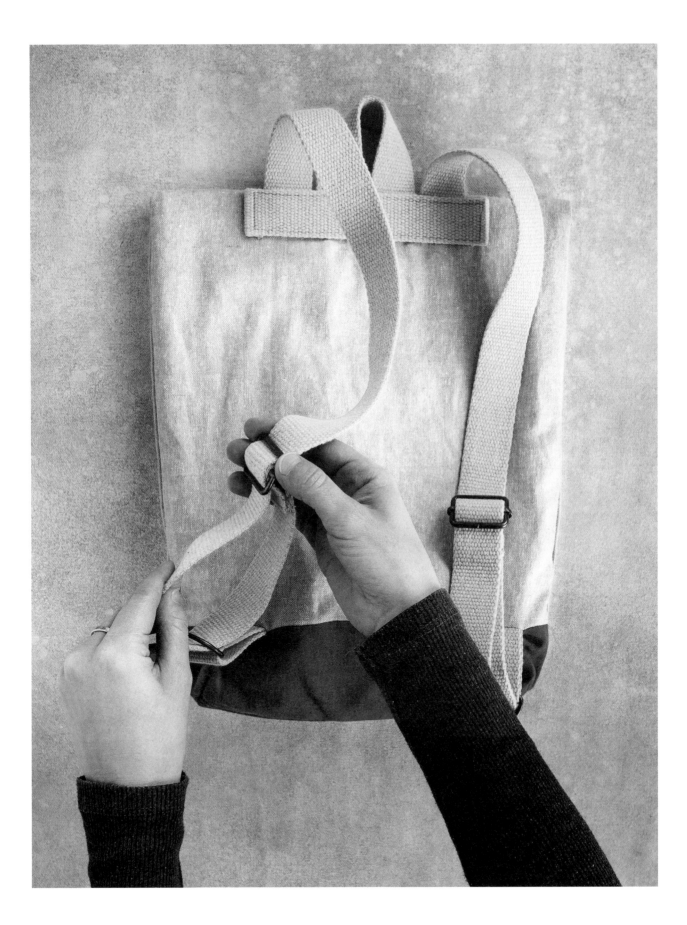

6 Tuck one end of each strap under the strip pinned at the top of your panel, on either side of the loop. Pin in place.

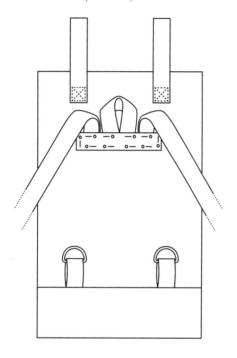

7 Thread the other end of one strap through the top of a strap adjuster from back to front, over the central bar and through to the back again, down and through the corresponding D-ring from front to back, then back up and over the central bar of the adjuster again as before – see Sliders and D-Rings on page 123 for more information. With about 4cm (1½in) of webbing coming out of the adjuster, fold the end under by 1cm (⅜in) and pin to the strap at the back to make a loop. Repeat this step for the second strap.

8 Sew the two loops closed with two rows of stitching (I also added a few stitches by hand at the sides to stop any frayed ends showing).

9 Return to the strip holding your loop and the tops of your straps in place. Sew all the way around, about 3mm (⅛in) in from the edge. Do this a couple of times to make it secure.

10 Lay the back panel of your backpack (the one you've just sewn the straps to) right side up and arrange the straps in the middle so they don't overlap the edges and get caught in the seams. Lay your front panel on top, right side down. Pin along the sides and bottom edge, then sew along those three edges with a 1cm (⅜in) seam allowance.

11 Square off the bottom corners of your bag by flattening the corner and sewing a line 3cm (1¼in) from the corner of the seam – see Squaring Corners on pages 124–125 for more information. Turn right side out.

12 Repeat steps 10 and 11 with your lining but don't turn it right side out.

13 Slip your lining piece into your main bag and line up the seams. Fold the main bag top edge in and the top edge of the lining over to the wrong side (so the folded parts are facing each other), both by 1cm (⅜in) all the way around, and pin together. Sew all the way around the top edge about 3mm (⅛in) in from the edge.

14 Following the instructions in the kit, add the positive snap halves to your closure tabs about 6cm (2⅜in) from the ends, making sure the caps are on the front. I find it useful to use a bradawl or similar sharp tool to make a small hole first.

15 Fold the top of your bag over by about 9cm (3½in), so that the strip holding the loop and straps is at the top of the back. Check your tabs are both roughly the same distance from the side edges and mark where the snaps meet the front of your bag. This is where the negative halves of your snaps will need to go.

16 Add the other halves of your snaps to the front of your bag, where you've marked, making sure the caps are on the inside of your bag.

DESIGN NOTE

The colour contrasts between the main and base fabrics and the straps/tabs is key to making this design work. I like to use a fairly neutral colour for the main fabric, something a bit darker to give the base a feeling of weight and then something bright or strong for the straps and tabs as highlights.

Occasions

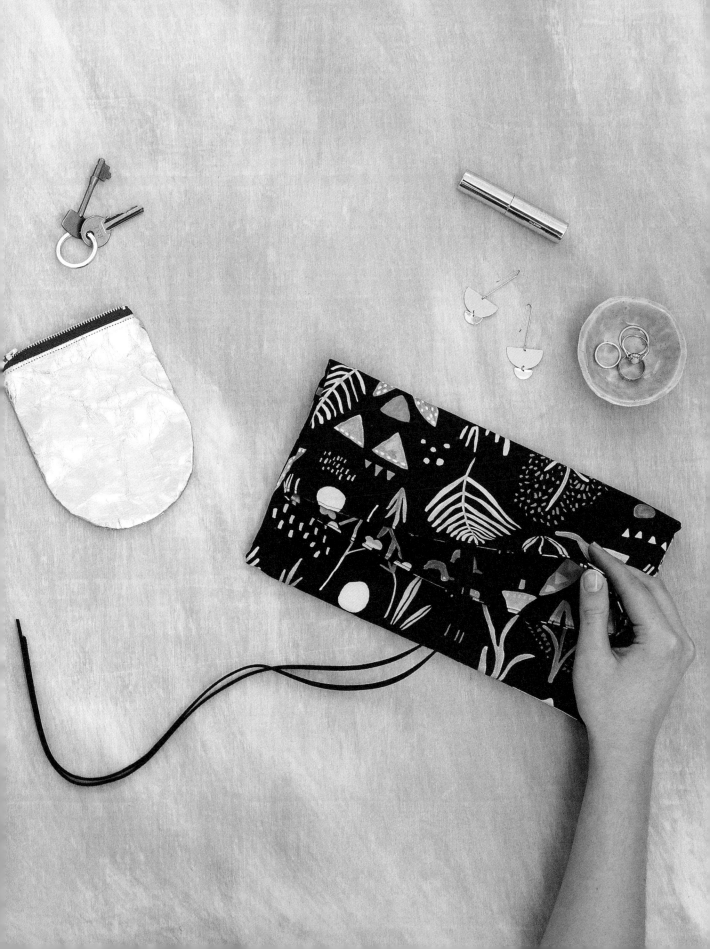

Curved Purse

So you've made yourself a beautiful bag (or maybe six!), but now that means your tatty old purse is really not cutting it any more... This curvy little one will fix that for you. The larger version can double as a small clutch for those times when you really only need your phone and card, or a handy little makeup bag! The materials and instructions are for one purse, either large or small.

QUICK MAKE

Skill level ●○○

Materials

¼m (⅜yd) medium-weight canvas OR ¼m (18 x 22in) washable paper fabric

To give your paper fabric a crinkly, vintage leather look and make it softer to work with, simply pop it through the washing machine at 40°C (100°F) and then leave to dry!

¼m (⅜yd) lining fabric

15cm (6in) metallic zip (for large purse) OR 12cm (5in) zip (for small purse)

Thread to match your fabric

Basic sewing kit

Cut out

For large purse

MAIN FABRIC

Two pieces: **Template A** (see page 134)

LINING FABRIC

Two pieces: **Template A**

For small purse

MAIN FABRIC

Two pieces: **Template B** (see page 134)

LINING FABRIC

Two pieces: **Template B**

The metallic zip, and especially the gold washable paper, elevate this simple pattern to something quite special.

1   Lay out one of your lining pieces right side up. Place your zip right side up on top, so that its edge lines up with the straight edge of your lining. Then lay one of your main fabric pieces right side down on top, lining up the edges – see Inserting Zips on pages 126–127 for more information.

2   Pin (or use fabric clips if you're working with paper fabric) along the top straight edge about 5mm (¼in) from the edge.

3   Using a zipper foot on your machine, sew along the edge you've pinned, about 3mm (⅛in) from where you can feel the zip's teeth.

4   Fold your pieces of fabric back the other way so they are wrong sides together and you can see your zip.

5   Lay your other lining piece out right side up and place your zip right side up on top again, with its unsewn edge along the straight edge of your lining. Place your other main fabric piece right side down on top, pin and then sew as before.

6   Open out and fold this side, as you did with the other side, so that all your fabric pieces are now right side out. Press along the seams (if using paper fabric, place a cloth or clean tea-towel over your fabric before ironing).

7   Pin and then sew along both straight edges of your fabric only (don't forget to change your machine's foot back first), about 2mm (¹⁄₁₆in) from the seams.

8   Fold your fabrics right sides together again, but this time so that the two main fabric pieces are facing, as are the two lining pieces.

9   Unzip your zip!

10 Pin/clip all the way around the curved edges, 1cm (⅜in) from the edge. Make sure the zip's teeth are pointing towards the lining side (I always start by pinning where the ends of the zip are to get them pointing the right way).

11 Sew all the way around the edge with a 1cm (⅜in) seam allowance, but leaving a 6cm (2⅜in) gap on the lining side (leave a 10cm (4in) gap if using paper fabric).

12 If you're using fabric, snip roughly 8mm (⁵⁄₁₆in) cuts along the curved edges about every 1.5cm (⅝in) – this prevents the curves bunching up when you turn them out – see snipping Curved Edges on page 130 for more information. If using paper fabric, trim the seam to 5mm (¼in).

13 Turn right side out through the gap. Sew up the gap (it'll be hidden inside the purse so you can do this with your machine or by hand).

14 Tuck the lining back through the zip and give your purse a press.

FABRIC NOTE

As both versions of this purse are quite petite I've relied on using fabric with a bit of body (medium-weight canvas and washable paper) rather than interfacing. If you have a lightweight fabric you'd love to use instead, just add some light interfacing to the lining.

Interview Bag

Not every occasion calls for a tiny clutch bag or something sparkly – sometimes you need a bag that's about helping you feel organized and confident. This bag is understated but with touches of luxury (like the faux leather handles with gold details), and its inner divide keeps everything organized but easily accessible – exactly what you need for that big interview!

Skill level ●●●

Materials

¾m (⅝yd) tinted denim fabric (or similar heavy-weight twill or canvas)

½m (⅝yd) quilting-weight cotton for lining

½m (⅝yd) stiff fusible interfacing

1½m (1¾yd) faux leather strap, 3cm (1¼in) wide (I've used faux leather straps which are backed with webbing for a sturdy, high-quality feel)

Depending on the type of strap you are using you may need to seal the cut ends by carefully running a lighter flame quickly along them; this melts the ends slightly and stops fraying (unraveling) – check the details of the strapping when you buy it.

8 Chicago screws, 1cm (⅜in) across, 5mm (¼in) shaft height

Bradawl

Thread to match your fabric

Basic sewing kit

Cut out

MAIN FABRIC

Two pieces: 38cm (15in) high x 34cm (13⅜in) wide

One piece: 62cm (24⅜in) high x 25cm (10in) wide for divider

LINING FABRIC

Two pieces: 38cm (15in) high x 34cm (13⅜in) wide

INTERFACING

Two pieces: 38cm (15in) high x 34cm (13⅜in) wide

One piece: 31cm (12¼in) high x 25cm (10in) wide for divider

STRAP

Two pieces: 65cm (25½in) long

FABRIC NOTE

I chose to keep the outer fabric plain and smart while using a gorgeously patterned fabric for the lining – it's a bit like having a little secret luxury inside the bag to make you smile every time you open it!

1   Let's start by making the divider. Fold the divider fabric piece in half, right side out, so the shorter edges meet, and press. Slide the interfacing divider piece between the folded layers and press to fuse.

2   Take your two lining fabric pieces and mark and cut out a 4.5cm (1¾in) square hole out of each bottom corner.

3   Lay out one of your lining pieces right side up and with the cut out corners at the bottom. Place your divider piece on top (with its folded edge towards the top), aligning it with the right-hand edge and with its bottom right-hand corner aligned with the top of the cut-out in the lining bottom right-hand corner.

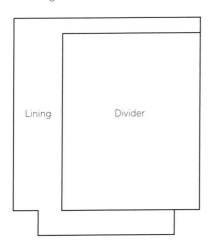

4   Lay the other lining piece right side down on top, matching up all the edges with the first lining piece. Pin along the right-hand edge only, 1cm (⅜in) in from the edge.

5   Next, line up the left-hand edge of the divider with the left-hand edge of the lining pieces (above the cut-out corner as before) and pin as you did for the right. You'll need to bunch up the lining pieces a bit to do this.

6   Sew along both the edges you pinned with a 1cm (⅜in) seam allowance, stopping 1cm (⅜in) above the cut-out squares.

7   Bring the bottom edges of both pieces of lining fabric level with the bottom edge of the divider (as before, you'll need to bunch the lining up a bit to do this), and pin along that bottom edge. Sew along that edge with a 1cm (⅜in) seam allowance.

8   To finish the lining, flatten it so the side seam is on top of the bottom seam, which will flatten the corner so the edges of the little square you cut out will now be in a straight line – see Squaring Corners on pages 124–125 for more information. Pin along that edge and sew with a 1cm (⅜in) seam allowance. Repeat for the other corner.

9   Now place your two main fabric pieces right side down, and lay an interfacing piece on top of each (see page 122 for more information on interfacing). Press to fuse.

10 Cut out 4.5cm (1¾in) squares from the bottom corners of both of your main pieces, as you did with the lining.

DESIGN NOTE

I've use Chicago screws here to create a really professional, finished look, but without having to invest in the tools that are often needed to fit metal findings. If you really get into making bags then you might want to invest in various leather punches and tools, but Chicago screws are a great way to start.

11 Lay out one of your main pieces right side up and place the other on top right side down. Pin and sew the side and bottom edges (but not around the cut-out squares) with a 1cm (⅜in) seam allowance.

12 Flatten the bottom corners as you did for the lining, then pin and sew with a 1cm (⅜in) seam allowance.

13 Turn your main bag right side out, fold the top edge in by 1cm (⅜in) and then press.

14 Slip your lining into the main bag, matching up the side seams. Fold the lining top edge by about 1.2cm (½in) over to the wrong side (so the folded part is facing the folded edge of the main bag). Pin the two edges together all the way around, with the lining sitting about 2mm (1⁄16in) below the main fabric.

15 Sew all the way around the top edge, about 4mm (3⁄16in) in, securing the lining in place.

16 Lastly, we need to add the handles. At one end of one of your straps mark a point 1.5cm (⅝in) up from the cut edge and centred between the long edges. Make another mark 2.5cm (1in) from the cut edge and in the centre. Punch a 4mm (3⁄16in) hole (check this is the right size for the shaft of your particular Chicago screws). I've used a bradawl to punch the holes but you could also use a leather hole-punch if you have one.

17 Repeat step 16 at the other end of that strap and at both ends of the second strap.

18 Measure 9.5cm (3¾in) in from the right-hand edge of your bag and 1.5cm (⅝in) down from the top edge and mark a point. Measure 9.5cm (3¾in) in from the side again and this time 4cm (1½in) down from the top edge. At both these points punch a hole as you did on your straps.

19 Repeat this on the left-hand side of your bag, then turn your bag over and repeat on the other side, on both the left and right.

20 Take one of your handles and line up the punched holes at one end over one set of punched holes on your bag. Push the front piece (the one without the screw top) of a Chicago screw through each of the holes in that end of your strap and through the holes in the bag. Screw on the back piece of each Chicago screw until secure.

21 Repeat step 20 with the other end of the same handle on the same side of the bag. Then add the handle on the other side of the bag in the same way.

Day-to-evening Bag

This is the bag for those times when you're going straight out after work – you need something big enough to stash your comfy shoes in but still lovely enough to feel special!

Skill level ●●○

Materials

½m (⅝yd) metallic jacquard fabric (or similar medium-weight fabric)

½m (⅝yd) heavy-weight canvas for lining

Two 34cm (13⅜in) long wooden dowels, about 1cm (⅜in) diameter

Use a hand saw to cut your dowels down if they are longer than specified.

Thread to match your fabric

Rotary cutter

Rotary compass circle cutter

Cutting mat

Seam ripper

Basic sewing kit

Cut out

MAIN FABRIC

Two pieces: 42cm (16½in) x 42cm (16½in)

LINING FABRIC

Two pieces: 42cm (16½in) x 42cm (16½in)

_____

FABRIC NOTE

I've used a stunning jacquard fabric for this bag, which has both texture and metallic threads. It would also look awesome in some lovely washable paper fabric or even faux leather.

_____

1   Lay out your two main fabric squares right side up and then lay a lining square on top of each (right side down if they have a right side).

2   Pin and sew around 1cm (⅜in) in from the edges, leaving a 6cm (2⅜in) gap on one edge (the bottom edge if your fabric has a directional pattern). Snip diagonally across the corners of the seam allowance.

3   Turn your two squares right side out through the gap and press (you don't need to sew up the opening).

4   Lay one of your squares out with the main fabric right side down, and with the gap on the bottom edge. From the top edge, measure 4cm (1½in) down and mark a line in tailor's chalk all the way across. Mark the centre point of that line.

5   Set your rotary compass cutter to an 8cm (3⅛in) radius and, placing the point of the compass on the centre mark you made, cut a semi-circle below your line through both layers of fabric.

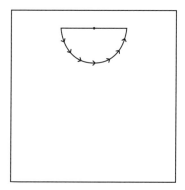

6   Use your straight rotary cutter to cut across the top of your semi-circle through both layers of fabric, so your semi-circle is completely cut out. Remove and discard the semi-circles of fabric.

7   Snip 8mm (⁵⁄₁₆in) long cuts roughly every 1cm (⅜in) around the curved edge of your semi-circle through both layers of fabric – see snipping Curved Edges on page 130 for more information. Make the same length diagonal cuts at the corners.

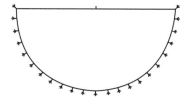

8   Turn your fabric square over. Fold the edges of the main fabric and lining in by 1cm (⅜in) so they meet face to face all the way around your semi-circle, including its straight edge, pinning as you go.

9   Sew all around your cut-out area 2mm (¹⁄₁₆in) in from the edge.

10 Repeat steps 4 to 9 for your other panel.

11 Lay one of your panels out with the main fabric right side up and lay the other with the main fabric right side down on top, so the semi-circles match up on the top edge, and pin together along the sides and bottom edge. On the right-hand side, starting 7cm (2¾in) down from the top edge, sew along that edge with about an 8mm (⁵⁄₁₆in) seam allowance. Continue sewing along the bottom edge and then up the left-hand edge, stopping 7cm (2¾in) from the top edge on that side too.

12 Turn your bag right side out.

13 At the very top of the right-hand edge, use your seam ripper to unpick about 2cm (¾in) of the seam on both your panels. Insert one of your dowels along the top edge of each panel.

14 Where your side seams are open – so the top 7cm (2¾in) left open in step 11 on both sides – fold in each edge along the seamline by about 1cm (⅜in) and hand sew in place, sewing up the gaps you unpicked as you go.

15 Press your bag.

DESIGN NOTE

I decided to hide the dowel handles within the structure of the bag, so you get the benefit of their sturdy strength in holding the shape of the bag, but the design remains elegant.

Fold-over Clutch

This modern clutch is super simple and quick to make – perfect to whip up when you can't find just the right bag for your outfit!

QUICK MAKE

Skill level ●○○

Materials

¾m (⅞yd) medium-weight canvas fabric

½m (⅝yd) stiff fusible interfacing

1m (1⅛yd) faux suede cord, around 3mm (⅛in) diameter

Thread to match your fabric

Basic sewing kit

Cut out

MAIN FABRIC
Four pieces: 30cm (12in) x 30cm (12in)

INTERFACING
Two pieces: 30cm (12in) x 30cm (12in)

FAUX SUEDE CORD
Two pieces: 50cm (19¾in) long

FABRIC NOTE
A medium-weight canvas is ideal for this bag as it has a bit of weight and stiffness for a crisp look.

FABRIC NOTE

Many fabrics have a pattern that works either way up, so you can make both front and back of your bag with the fabric in the same direction and it will still work when the top is folded over, but if your fabric happens to have a pattern that has a distinct single direction you might want to place your second outer piece so that the pattern is upside down. This means that when the 'back' of the bag is folded over, the pattern will appear right way up.

1   Lay out two of your main fabric squares right side down and lay an interfacing square on top of each, shiny side down. Following the instructions for your particular interfacing, press with a hot iron to fuse the interfacing to the fabric (see page 122 for more information on interfacing). These interfaced pieces will be your lining.

2   Lay out one of your remaining main fabric squares right side up and lay one of your interfaced lining pieces right side down on top (for both pieces make sure your fabric pattern is the right way up, i.e. it looks right as it is laid out in front of you). Pin and then sew along the top edge with a 1cm (⅜in) seam allowance.

3   Repeat with the other remaining canvas square and lining piece, but this time before sewing the top edge add your cords. To do this, mark the middle point of your top edge then place the two cords together between the two layers of fabric, so that one end of both cords sticks out a little at the centre mark you made. Pin the cords in place before sewing along the top edge with a 1cm (⅜in) seam allowance.

4   Open out both your lining/outer pairs and press to flatten along the seams. Fold each pair again but this time so each has wrong sides together. Press, then pin along the top (sewn) edge close to the seam. Finally, sew along the top (seam) edge 2mm (⅛in) in from the edge.

5   Once again, unfold your pairs and press. Now lay out one opened-out pair right side up and lay the other pair on top right side down, making sure the two outer pieces are facing and so are the lining (interfaced) pieces. Pin all the way around the edges (making sure the cords don't get caught).

6   Sew all the way around with a 1cm (⅜in) seam allowance, but leaving a 6cm (2⅜in) gap on one of the lining edges. Snip the seam allowance diagonally across the corners, close to your stitching.

7   Turn your bag right side out through the gap. Sew up the gap (this will be hidden inside the bag, so you can do this with your machine).

8   Push the lining down into the outer and press.

9   Fold the open end of your clutch over by roughly 10cm (4in) and wrap your cords around the clutch to hold it closed.

DESIGN NOTE

I decided to add faux suede ties as the closure here to add a modern, slightly-less-tidy edge to a classic clutch shape.

Contrast Clutch

Patchwork may not be the most modern of techniques, but here it's used to create a striking and distinctly up-to-date clutch. The relationship between the two colours you choose is key, so grab some swatches and play about until you get it just right!

Skill level ●●○

Materials

¼m (⅜yd) plain quilting-weight cotton fabric

¼m (⅜yd) plain quilting-weight cotton in a contrast colour

¼m (⅜yd) stiff fusible interfacing

1 magnetic fastening, about 18mm (¾in) wide

Thread to match your fabric

Basic sewing kit

Cut out

MAIN FABRIC

One piece: 18.5cm (7¼in) high x 28cm (11in) wide for back

One piece: **Template A** (see inside the back cover) for front

One piece: **Template C** (see inside the back cover) for front

CONTRAST FABRIC

Two pieces: 18.5cm (7¼in) high x 28cm (11in) wide for lining

One piece: **Template B** (see inside the back cover) for contrast flash

INTERFACING

Two pieces: 18.5cm (7¼in) high x 28cm (11in) wide

FABRIC NOTE

Stiff, thin interfacing (combined with quilting-weight fabrics) is ideal for this clutch as it gives structure without adding bulk that would detract from the sharp lines.

1   Place your lining pieces right side down, and lay an interfacing piece on top of each, shiny side down. Press the interfacing to fuse as per the instructions for your particular interfacing (see page 122 for more information on interfacing).

2   Measure and mark a point on each of your lining/interfacing pieces 3cm (1¼in) down from one of the longer edges and centred between the two shorter edges. At the point you've marked, add the positive side of your magnet fastening to one lining/interfacing piece and the negative side to the other piece, following the instructions on the packet. Set your lining/interfacing pieces aside for now.

3   Lay out the three fabric shapes you cut using the templates (see inside the back cover), right side up, matching up both edges marked X, and both edges marked Y as shown.

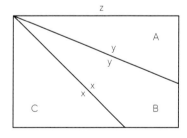

4   Turn piece **C** over on to piece **B** along edge X. Pin along that edge then sew with a 1cm (⅜in) seam allowance. Unfold and press the seam flat.

5   Lay out your pieces again and turn piece **A** over on to piece **B** along edge Y. Pin and then sew with a 1cm (⅜in) seam allowance, as before. Unfold and press.

6   Lay out your finished patchwork panel right side up, and so that edge Z is at the top. Place the lining/interfacing piece with the positive side of the magnet fastening on top, right side down, and so the fastening is towards the top edge. Pin and sew along the top edge only with a 1cm (⅜in) seam allowance.

7   Take your other outer fabric piece and lay out right side up. Place your second lining/interfacing piece right side down on top as before, with the magnet fastening towards the top edge. Pin and sew along the top edge with a 1cm (⅜in) seam allowance, as before.

8   Open out both your pieces and press flat. Lay out the pieces right sides together, making sure the two outer pieces are facing and the two lining pieces are facing. Pin all the way around the edges. Sew around the edges with a 1cm (⅜in) seam allowance, leaving a 6cm (2⅜in) gap on one of the lining edges.

9   Turn your clutch right side out through the gap and then machine or hand sew the gap closed.

10 Finally, tuck your lining down into the outer bag and give your clutch a press.

DESIGN NOTE

To keep the lines of this clutch really clean,
I've used a magnet fastening, so there's no zip
or clasp showing.

Pompom Bucket Bag

Striking and fun – but still big enough to hold all your essentials!
I love the idea of this bag turning heads at a non-traditional
wedding, a picnic birthday party or a festival.

Skill level ●●○

Materials

Small, unlined canvas rug or ½m
(⅝yd) heavy-weight canvas fabric

½m (⅝yd) quilting-weight cotton
for lining

10 eyelets, 1cm (⅜in) across,
with eyelet tool (you can buy
this as a little kit)

1m (1⅛yd) cotton cord,
3mm (⅛in) diameter

1m (1⅛yd) webbing,
2cm (¾in) wide

1 ball of yarn in each of two colours

I used a DK-weight cotton yarn for the
pompoms and tassels, but you could use
any yarn you like and experiment with the
kind of pompoms and tassels it creates.

Thread to match your rug/fabric

4.5cm (1¾in) pompom maker

Hammer to fit eyelets

Pen or pencil

Basic sewing kit

Cut out

MAIN FABRIC/RUG

One piece: 28cm (11in) high
x 51.5cm (20¼in) wide

One piece: Template circle
(see page132)

LINING FABRIC

One piece: 28cm (11in) high
x 51.5cm (20¼in) wide

One piece: Template circle

WEBBING

One length: 90cm (35½in)
for strap

One length: 8cm (3⅛in)
for cord toggle

I wanted the pompoms to stand out as a pop of colour, so I chose a black and white fabric so they wouldn't be competing with other colours.

1   Lay your main fabric piece out right side up, in a landscape position, and fold so the shorter edges meet. Pin and then sew along that edge with a 1cm (⅜in) seam allowance to make a tube.

2   Take your main circle piece and pin it, right sides together, to the bottom edge of your tube, about 1cm (⅜in) in (no matter how carefully I measure, I always need to adjust this a little to get the circle to fit just right, so don't worry if you have to move the pins a little further in or out). Sew around the edge of your circle piece, with about a 1cm ⅜in) seam allowance.

3   Turn your bag right side out.

4   Repeat steps 1 and 2 with your lining fabrics, but don't turn right side out.

5   Slip your lining into your main bag, matching up the seam. Fold the top edge of your main fabric in by about 1.5cm (⅝in) and the top edge of your lining over by 2cm (¾in) to the wrong side (so the folded part is facing the folded edge of the main bag). Pin together, so the edge of the lining is about 5mm (¼in) below the edge of the main fabric.

6   With your seam at the centre of the back, mark the middle point on either side of your bag. Take your long length of webbing and tuck one end between the outer and lining layers by about 2cm (¾in) at one of the points you marked. Tuck in the other end in the same way at the other point, checking your webbing isn't twisted first. Pin the ends of your webbing in place.

7   Sew all the way around the top of your bag about 2mm (⅟₁₆in) below the top edge of the lining.

8   Now it's time to add your eyelets. Starting from the point where one end of your strap meets your bag, measure and mark 10 points at 5cm (2in) intervals around the top of your bag, each 2.5cm (1in) down from the top edge.

9   Following the instructions on your eyelet kit, fit an eyelet, right side out, at each of the points you have marked.

10 Thread your cord front-to-back through one of your eyelets at the front of your bag (i.e. with the seam at the back and the strap to either side). Continue threading in and out through the eyelets until your cord comes out of the eyelet next to the one you started with.

11 For the cord toggle, lay out your short length of webbing and fold one cut edge over by 2cm (¾in) and the other over by 1cm (⅜in) then again by 2cm (¾in). Pin along the centre. Sew two lines along the centre, 5mm (¼in) apart. This will have created a small channel at either side (it can help to open these out by pushing a pencil through them).

12 Thread each end of your cord through one of the channels on the toggle you made.

13 Now it's time to make the tassels and pompoms. Let's start with the tassels – first cut a strand of yarn about 25cm (10in) long and set aside. Hold your hand (whichever isn't your writing hand) out flat and begin wrapping your yarn around your fingers. Once you have wrapped it enough times to form a nice full tassel, slide the looped yarn off your fingers. At one end, slide a pencil through the loop you've made. Then, slip your scissors through the loop at the other end and cut the strands. Gather your strands of wool tightly together below the pencil, take the strand of wool you cut earlier and tie it tightly just below the pencil. Wrap the ends in opposite directions around your tassel, just below the pencil, and then tie off. Trim your tassel so the cut ends are all level. Repeat for a second tassel.

14 Slide one of your tassels off its pencil and thread your bag's cord through the hole where the pencil was. Tie the cord to hold the tassel in place (the knot will be hidden later). You might want to add a few stitches to the knot just to make it extra secure. Repeat for the other end of the cord and the other tassel.

15 Finally, it's time to add your pompoms! Take your pompom maker and, following the instructions (different pompom makers may have slightly different instructions), wrap one of its sides with your yarn. Close that side and wrap the second side. Before closing, lay one of your cords at right angles across the middle section of the pompom maker so it will be trapped as you close the second side (you'll slide your pompom into place later, so it doesn't need to be right at the end of your cord). Close the pompom maker over the cord, then snip the strands of yarn around the edge of your pompom maker. Take an extra length of yarn and tie it tightly around the middle of the pompom maker, pulling it into the groove. Open out and remove the pompom maker. Slide your pompom into place at the end of your cord (it should overlap the top of your tassel a little and cover the knot holding your tassel in place). Trim your pompom to make it neat and round. Repeat on the other cord.

FABRIC NOTE

I was thinking about summer bags when I designed this, especially the chunkier textures of straw bags. To get that feel, but using an easy-to-sew fabric, I wanted a canvas with a really bold, chunky weave – I actually ended up using a small canvas rug as the pattern and texture were just what I was looking for!

Travel

Drawstring Toiletries Bag

If you're not the kind of person who can get by with just a sachet of shampoo for a week's holiday, this is the toiletries bag for you! With six internal pockets to hold your kit in place and padding to keep everything safe, this bag should do the trick.

Skill level ●●○

Materials

½m (⅝yd) patterned quilting-weight cotton

A fat quarter will do for this but some shops only cut full widths, in which case you'll need ½m (⅝yd).

¾m (⅞yd) plain quilting-weight cotton for lining and pockets

¾m (⅞yd) light-weight quilt wadding (I prefer natural fibres such as cotton or bamboo)

1m (1⅛yd) cotton cord, 5mm (¼in) diameter

2 metal caps for 5mm (¼in) cord

Superglue

Thread to match your fabric

Basic sewing kit

Cut out

MAIN FABRIC

One piece: 52cm (20½in) wide x 38cm (15in) high

LINING FABRIC

One piece: 52cm (20½in) wide x 35cm (13¾in) high

One piece: 71cm (28in) wide x 32cm (12½in) high, for pockets

WADDING (BATTING)

One piece: 52cm (20½in) wide x 36.5cm (14⅜in) high

One piece: 71cm (28in) wide x 16cm (6¼in) high, for pockets

FABRIC NOTE

This bag is made using quilting-weight cottons and wadding (batting), and could be hand-washed if you have any spills. If you want to make totally sure you won't end up with shampoo all over your luggage, you could also add a layer of light waterproof fabric (such as ripstop) to the back of the lining.

1   Start by preparing your main fabric piece for the drawstring channel we'll make later. Lay out your main piece right side down, in a landscape position. At one of the top corners fold a narrow triangle in from the side, 5mm (¼in) wide by about 4cm (1½in) long, then fold over again by the same amount and pin – see Drawstrings step 1 on page 121 for more information. Repeat on the other top corner. Sew along the inner edges of both of your little triangles. Set your main fabric piece aside for now.

2   To make the pockets, take your pocket piece in lining fabric and fold in half with right sides together (if it has a right side) so that the long edges meet, then press the crease with your iron. Lay this strip on top of your pocket wadding (batting) piece. Pin along both long edges of the strip and then sew along those edges with a 5mm (¼in) seam allowance. Now fold right side out, so that the wadding ends up in the middle. Sew along both long edges again, 8mm (⅝in) in from the edge.

3   Lay out your main lining piece right side up and in a landscape position and place your pocket strip on top, 10cm (4in) up from the bottom long edge, with its right-hand short edge lining up exactly with the right-hand edge of the main lining piece.

4   To make your pockets, first pin the right-hand edges together, then bunch up your pocket strip and pin at roughly 8cm intervals as shown on the diagram. I made some of the pockets quite flat and some quite curvy to accommodate a range of different containers. You can vary the number and sizes of the pockets to suit yourself if you'd like.

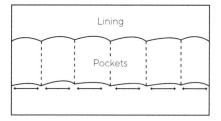

5   Sew from top to bottom of the pocket piece where you've pinned to create your pockets (these will stay open at the top and bottom).

6   Fold your lining piece in half so that the short edges meet and the pockets are on the inside. Pin, then sew along the side and bottom edges with a 1cm (⅜in) seam allowance, leaving the top edge open.

7   Flatten one of the bottom corners so the side-seam or crease is over the bottom seam, pin and then sew across it 6.25cm (2½in) from the tip of the corner – see Squaring Corners on pages 124–125 for more information. Repeat on the other bottom corner. Leave wrong side out.

8   Lay your main fabric out right side down, with the turned-over corners at the top. Lay your matching piece of wadding (batting) on top so that the bottom long edge of each aligns. Pin and then sew along the top and bottom long edges of your wadding (batting) with a 5mm (¼in) seam allowance.

9 Turn your main/wadding piece over so that the main fabric is right side up and fold in half with right sides together so that the short edges meet. Pin and sew along the side and bottom (but not the top) edges with a 1cm (⅜in) seam allowance.

10 Square the bottom corners off as you did in step 7 for the lining.

11 Turn your main piece right side out then tuck your lining piece down inside it, lining up the seams and corners.

12 Fold the main bag top edge in by 2.5cm (1in) and the lining top edge over by 1cm (⅜in) to the wrong side (so the folded part is facing the folded edge of the main bag), pinning in place together. Sew around the top of the lining, 2–3mm (⅛in) in from the folded edges – this should be roughly 1.5cm (⅝in) from the top of the main piece's edge.

13 Insert your cord using safety pins to help you thread it through the channel – see Drawstrings step 2 on page 121 for more information if you're not familiar with adding drawstrings.

14 Trim your cord so that there's at least 5cm (2in) of each end showing when the bag is fully opened.

15 Glue an end cap to each end of your cord and leave to dry.

16 To close your bag, pull the drawstrings tight and tie in a single knot.

DESIGN NOTE

As this isn't a bag you'll wear, you don't have to worry about the colours or patterns suiting your wardrobe, so it's a nice chance to go for a more quirky fabric or unusual colours.

Foldaway Drawstring

This is a great little bag to pop in your luggage for when you want something light but practical to stash away your daily essentials while exploring somewhere new!

QUICK MAKE

Skill level ●●○

Materials

½m (⅝yd) patterned quilting-weight cotton fabric

½m (⅝yd) plain quilting-weight cotton fabric for lining

3m (3⅜yd) cotton cord, about 5mm (¼in) diameter

Thread to match your fabrics

Two safety pins

Basic sewing kit

Cut out

MAIN FABRIC
One piece: 68cm (26¾in) high x 29cm (11½in) wide

LINING FABRIC
One piece: 68cm (26¾in) high x 29cm (11½in) wide

CORD
Two pieces: 150cm (59in) long

1   Lay out the main piece right side down and at the top and bottom of each long side, fold over a narrow triangle, twice, about 5mm (¼in) wide and 6cm (2⅜in) long – see Drawstrings step 1 on page 121 for more information. Pin, then sew in place. Do the same with your lining piece.

2   Lay out the main piece right side up, and lay the lining piece on top right side down. Pin and then sew along both shorter edges only with a 1cm (⅜in) seam allowance. Trim the seams to 5mm (¼in) and oversew with a zigzag stitch.

3   Turn your tube of fabric right side out and press along the sewn edges. Now pin and sew 1.5cm (⅝in) from the seam at both short ends, creating two channels for your cord.

4   Turn your fabric tube wrong side out again. The two cord channels will be on the inside, so bring them to meet in the centre of your tube, one on top of the other, and then flatten the tube so that the lining fabric is folded above the centre and main fabric is folded below it – making sure that the cord channels are both lying towards the lining fabric. Give your fabric a press.

5   Pin a safety pin to the end of one cord and use it to help thread the cord through one of your channels, then back through the other channel. Repeat in the opposite direction

with the second piece of cord (so you end up with two strands of cord coming out at each side). Make sure the cords coming out of the channels are all roughly the same length by pulling the cords to adjust, and make sure your channels are smooth, not bunched up.

6   Take the two strands of cord that are extending at the right-hand end of the channels and push them between the two layers of patterned fabric. Keeping the two ends together, tuck them right down into the bottom right-hand corner of the patterned fabric piece, but so that the ends extend out of the corner by 1cm (⅜in). Pin them in place. Repeat with the cords on the other side.

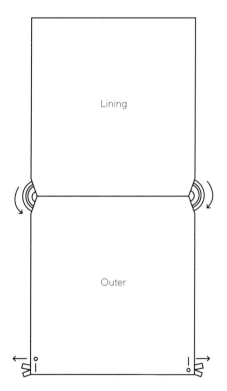

FABRIC NOTE

Lightweight fabric (such as quilting cotton) works well to keep this bag compact. You could also use a waterproof fabric, such as ripstop, for the outer layer to make it an all-weather bag!

7 Pin along the sides of your patterned piece, making sure the main lengths of cords are safely tucked out of the way inside (apart from the ends sticking out at the bottom corners), and checking the seams between lining and outer fabric match up along the centre.

8 Sew along the sides of your patterned fabric with a 1cm (⅜in) seam allowance, sewing as close as possible up to the cord channels (the thickness of the cords will stop you sewing right up to the channels, but you should be able to get pretty close).

9 Trim the cord where it sticks out at the bottom corners, then zigzag stitch over the seam allowance where the cord is sandwiched, to make it more secure.

10 Reaching inside the lining piece, fold the cord channels the other way, so they are tucked inside the patterned fabric side. Now pin and sew along the sides of the lining with a 1cm (⅜in) seam allowance, leaving a 6cm (2⅜in) gap along one side. As before, sew as close as you can up to the cord channels.

11 Turn your bag right side out though the gap you left. Fold the edges of the gap in by 1cm (⅜in) and sew it closed (you can do this by machine as it'll be hidden inside the bag).

12 Tuck your lining down into the patterned outer layer and pull on your drawstrings to close your bag!

DESIGN NOTE

As your fabric is folded to form the front and back of this bag it's important to choose a fabric with a pattern that works both ways up!

Oversized Beach Bag

Casual and roomy, this bag will be your go-to when you're carting bulky towels and spare clothes to the beach. It's also perfect for picnics in the park, shopping at the farmer's market or any time you need some serious capacity!

Skill level ●○○

Materials

½m (⅝yd) linen fabric

½m (⅝yd) linen fabric in a contrast colour

1m (1⅛yd) medium-weight canvas lining fabric

1m (1⅛yd) fusible interfacing strip, 2.5cm (1in) wide

Thread to match your fabrics

Basic sewing kit

Cut out

MAIN FABRIC

A One piece: 42cm (16½in) wide x 102cm (40⅛in) high

CONTRAST FABRIC

B Two pieces: 42cm (16½in) high x 22cm (8¾in) wide for sides

Two pieces: 50cm (19¾in) high x 12cm (4¾in) wide for handles

LINING FABRIC

One piece: 102cm (40⅛in) high x 42cm (16½in) wide

Two pieces: 42cm (16½in) high x 22cm (8¾in) wide

FABRIC NOTE

I wanted this bag to have a casual and relatively unstructured feel but still be strong enough for its generous size, so I chose soft but strong linen fabrics for the outer and a medium-weight canvas for a sturdy but not stiff lining.

1   Lay out the main fabric piece right side up, in a landscape position. Place one of your contrast side pieces right side down centred on top of the main piece. Pin in place and sew 1cm (⅜in) in along the bottom edge of the contrast piece, starting and stopping 1cm (⅜in) from each end.

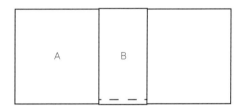

2   Turn the main piece around so the other long edge is facing you and fold the piece you just attached out of the way. Repeat step 1 with the second contrast side piece, so you end up with a contrast piece sewn at the centre of both long sides of the main piece.

3   Open out completely and press the seams flat.

4   With right sides together, bring the long edge of a contrast side piece to meet the corresponding part of the main piece's long edge (forming the bag's shape), pin then sew with a 1cm (⅜in) seam allowance. Repeat on the other edge and on the other contrast side piece. Trim the seam allowance diagonally across the corners to reduce bulk. Turn your outer bag right side out.

5   Repeat steps 1 to 4 with your lining fabric pieces, but don't turn right side out.

6   Tuck your lining into the outer bag so all the seams match up. Fold the edge of both pieces over to the wrong side by 1cm (⅜in) (so the folded pieces are right sides together), and pin together.

7   Before sewing the top edge we need to make the handles. Fold a handle strip in half so the two long edges meet and press. Unfold and then fold the long edges in to meet the crease along the middle, pressing again. Finally, re-fold along the middle so the long raw edges are concealed inside and press again – see Making Fabric Straps/Handles on pages 130–131 for more information. To strengthen the handle, add a strip of interfacing inside the folded layers and press to seal. Sew 2mm (⅛in) in along both long edges of the folded strip. Repeat with your other handle strip.

8   On the front of your bag measure 10cm (4in) in from the right seam and tuck in one end of one of handles by 2cm (¾in), pinning in place. Tuck the other end in 10cm (4in) from the left seam, making sure your handle isn't twisted. You might need to remove and replace some of the pins along your bag's top edge to do this.

9   Repeat step 8 on the other side of your bag with your second handle.

10 Finally, sew all the way around the top of your bag, 5mm (¼in) in from the edge. Now you're ready to hit the beach!

DESIGN NOTE

Using two different colours of the same fabric for this bag gives it contrast while keeping it looking clean and simple.

Boxy Hand-luggage

This travel bag is all about combining practicality – it's perfect hand-luggage size, although always check specific requirements for individual airlines – with a bit of luxury! I've also added a bag bottom (a special plastic panel) to reinforce the base.

Skill level ●●●

Materials

1m (1⅛yd) patterned medium-weight canvas fabric

1¼m (1⅜yd) plain medium-weight canvas fabric for lining

2m (2¼yd) foam interfacing

The amount required depends on the width because foam interfacing is usually much narrower than an average fabric width. Check the cut list for exactly how much you will need.

2½m (2¾yd) webbing, 2.5cm (1in) wide

At least 17cm (6¾in) x 51cm (20in) bag bottom

85cm (33½in) zip

120cm (47¼in) faux leather bag strap with swivel snap hooks

Thread to match your fabric and webbing

Basic sewing kit

Cut out

MAIN FABRIC

Two pieces: 50cm (19¾in) high x 86cm (33⅞in) wide

One piece: 60cm (24in) high x 21cm (8¼in) wide for pocket

Two pieces: 10cm (4in) high x 8cm (3⅛in) wide for strap loops

LINING FABRIC

Two pieces: 50cm (19¾in) high x 86cm (33⅞in) wide

Two pieces: 21cm (8¼in) high x 55cm (21⅝in) wide for base panel

INTERFACING

Two pieces: 50cm (19¾in) high x 86cm (33⅞in) wide

WEBBING

Two strips: 115cm (45¼in)

BAG BOTTOM

One piece: 19cm (7½in) high x 53cm (21in) wide for base panel

1   To prepare your strap loops, fold each piece in half so the long edges meet and press. Unfold and fold the long edges in to meet the crease, pressing again. Finally, fold in half again along the original crease. Sew along both long edges about 2mm (1⁄16in) in – see Making Fabric Straps/Handles on pages 130–131 for more information. Set aside for now.

2   For the handles, on each webbing strip measure and mark 45cm (17¾in) from each cut end. Working between the marks, fold and pin the webbing in half, so the long edges meet. Sew where you have pinned, 2mm (1⁄16in) in from the open edge – see Webbing Straps/Handles on page 129 for more information. Repeat with the other webbing strip. Set aside for now.

3   Lay out your interfacing pieces in a landscape position and lay your outer pieces right side up on top. Pin and sew all the way around the edges with a 5mm (¼in) seam allowance to secure the layers together.

4   Next, we'll add the pocket to one of these pieces. Fold your pocket piece in half with wrong sides together, so the shorter edges meet, and press. Sew along the folded edge (not the open edge) 2mm (1⁄16in) in from the fold. Lay your pocket piece on top of one of your outer/interfacing panels, so that the pocket's open bottom edges line up with the panel's bottom edge and the pocket is centred at the bottom of the panel. Pin and then sew along both sides of your pocket, 5mm (¼in) in from the edge. Measure and then sew across your pocket 12cm (4¾in) up from the bottom edge.

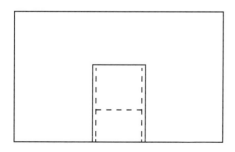

5   Next, measure and mark a line 30cm (12in) in from both right and left edges of your panel. Line up the outer edge of one webbing handle with the line on the right, lining up the cut end with the bottom edge of your panel. Pin your webbing in place then pin the other end so it lines up in the same way on the left-hand side (the webbing should also now cover the raw side edges of your pocket). Check the sewn edge of the centre part of your handle is facing downward. Starting at the bottom edge on the right-hand side, sew along the webbing about 2mm (1⁄16in) in from the edge, stopping 18cm (7in) from the top of the panel. Sew across the webbing, and then back down the other side. Repeat on the left-hand section of webbing.

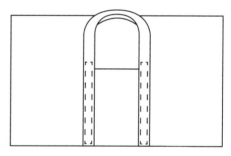

6   Repeat step 5 with your other handle strip and panel.

7   Fold both the handles back and pin out of the way of the panel edges.

8   Lay out one of your lining rectangles right side up, in a landscape position. Place your zip right side up, aligning the edge with the top of the lining. Lay one of your outer panels on top, right side down, and pin together along the top edge (make sure this is the edge where your handle will be). Using a zipper foot, sew along the pinned edge about 3mm (1⁄8in) from the zip's teeth – see Inserting Zips on pages 126–127 for more information.

DESIGN NOTE

This is one of the most structured bags in this book,
with the addition of a firm base insert to really
highlight the boxy shape.

FABRIC NOTE

I've used foam interfacing here, along with medium-weight canvas, to give this bag both a sturdy and a luxuriously padded feel.

9   Fold back the outer and lining panels so they are wrong sides together, revealing the zip, and press. Now repeat step 8 for the other edge of the zip with your remaining outer and lining rectangles. Again, fold back and press.

10   Change back to your regular sewing-machine foot and sew along either side of the zip, 5mm (¼in) from the seam.

11   Fold the fabric panels on either side of your zip together (keeping all the layers together), with the lining side facing out. Pin and then sew along the edge opposite to the zip with a 1cm (⅜in) seam allowance, leaving the side edges unsewn. Oversew along this seam with a zigzag stitch.

12   Open your panels out like a tube and flatten again the other way so the zip is now running along the centre and the seam you just sewed is directly below it (still with the lining facing out).

13   Unzip your zip!

14   Take one of your strap loop pieces and fold in half so the cut ends meet. Place this over the end of your zip, with the loop facing inwards and the cut ends sticking out over the end of the panel by 1cm (⅜in), and pin in place. Repeat with the other loop at the other end.

15   Pin and then sew along the open edges with a 1cm (⅜in) seam allowance. When you get to the zip teeth, lift your needle and push the work backwards in the machine slightly to jump over the teeth, then begin sewing again just on the other side.

16   Flatten one of the corners the other way, so it points towards you and the seam you just sewed runs up the centre away from you. Measure 14.5cm (5¾in) up from the tip of the corner and draw a line across the corner – see Squaring Corners on pages 124–125 for more information. Pin and then sew along this line. Trim away the corner 5mm (¼in) from the seam. Repeat for each of the other three corners.

17   Sew over all the raw edges with a wide zigzag stitch.

18   Turn your bag right way out and clip your long strap to the loops at either end of your zip.

19   To make your base panel, lay out the two lining fabric pieces right sides together and sew along both long and one short edge with a 1cm (⅜in) seam allowance. Turn right side out and then tuck your bag bottom insert inside. Fold the edges of the open end in by 1cm (⅜in) and hand sew closed. Tuck your base down inside your bag.

Retro Backpack

This style of trad backpack always takes me back to the late 80s, trying to make going back to school after summer slightly more bearable by stocking up on neon-themed stationery to fill my (probably also neon) backpack!

Skill level ●●●

Materials

½m (⅝yd) medium-weight cotton canvas

Join the two parts of **Template A** (see inside the back cover) into one piece before using it to cut the fabric.

¼m (18 x 22in) quilting-weight cotton for accent fabric

½m (⅝yd) quilting-weight cotton for lining

Thread to match your fabrics and webbing

40cm (16in) chunky zip

17cm (7in) regular zip (not a chunky zip)

2m (2¼yd) webbing, 2.5cm (1in) wide

2 D-rings, 2.5cm (1in) wide

2 sliding bar strap adjusters, 2.5cm (1in) wide

Basic sewing kit

Cut out

MAIN FABRIC

Two pieces: **Template A** (see inside the back cover) for front and back

Two pieces: 25cm (10in) high x 14cm (5½in) wide for sides

Two pieces: 13cm (5⅛in) high x 43cm (17in) wide for zip edges

One piece: 27cm (10⅝in) high x 14cm (5½in) wide for base

One piece: 26cm (10¼in) high x 21cm (8¼in) wide for pocket

Two pieces: 6cm (2⅜in) high x width of smaller zip for pocket zip tabs

ACCENT FABRIC

Two pieces: 25cm (10in) high x 14cm (5½in) wide for sides

One piece: 15cm (6in) high x 21cm (8¼in) wide for pocket flap

LINING FABRIC

Two pieces: **Template A** (see inside the back cover)

Two pieces: 25cm (10in) high x 14cm (5½in) wide for sides

One piece: 27cm (10⅝in) high x 14cm (5½in) wide for base

This design looks great in patterned or plain fabrics. For a more 80s retro feel choose an accent fabric that clashes a bit with your main fabric, or keep it subtle by picking out one of the colours from your main fabric.

1   Let's start by preparing the front pocket. Take your main pocket piece and fold it in half right sides together so the shorter edges meet, then pin together along the sides. Take your pocket flap piece (in the accent fabric) and fold right sides together, so the long edges meet. For both parts of your pocket, sew along the two shorter sides with a 1cm (⅜in) seam allowance, leaving the long open edge unsewn. Trim the seam allowance diagonally across the corners, turn right side out and press.

2   On both pieces, fold the open edge in by 1cm (⅜in) all the way around, press and sew along 2mm (¹⁄₁₆in) in from that edge.

3   Place one of your pocket zip tab pieces right side down and fold over the narrower edges by 1cm (⅜in), pressing to crease. Then fold the tab in half with wrong sides together so the folded edges meet, and press again. Repeat with the other tab.

4   Take your shorter zip and sandwich the tapes at one end between the two layers of a zip tab, then pin in place. Do the same at the other end of your zip. Make sure your zip is between 18cm (7in) and 18.5cm (7¼in) long in total, including the tabs (adjust the tabs or trim the zip down if needed). Sew across the zip tabs about 3mm (⅛in) from where they meet the zip teeth.

5   Lay out the zip you've been working on horizontally, right side up, and place your main pocket piece over the bottom tape, so that the folded long edge of your pocket piece is about 3mm (⅛in) from the zip's teeth. Check your zip is equidistant from both ends (the pocket panel should be slightly longer than the zip). Pin in place and then sew (using your machine's zipper foot) 2mm (¹⁄₁₆in) in.

6   Next, with the pocket piece below the zip and all still right side up, lay your flap piece on top of your zip so that the folded long edge overlaps the main pocket piece by 1cm (⅜in) (covering the zip). Pin along the top edge of the zip (you'll have to feel for this through the fabric), then sew about 3mm (⅛in) from the zip's teeth. You should now have a flat pocket panel made up of the pocket piece, zip and flap.

7   Now we can give the pocket its boxy shape. At each corner of your pocket panel cut out a 2cm (¾in) square. Now bring the edges

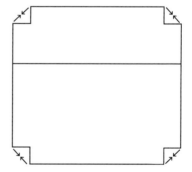

of one square opening together, right sides facing, pin and then sew with a 5mm (¼in) seam allowance (change back to a regular sewing foot) – see Squaring Corners on pages 124–125 for more information. Zigzag stitch over the seam allowance. Do the same with each of the remaining three corners. Push out the corners so that they are right side out.

8   Pin your pocket in place face-up centred on the front panel of your bag and 4.5cm (1¾in) up from the straight bottom edge. Sew around your pocket 2mm (⅟₁₆in) in from the edge. (This can be a bit fiddly, as your pocket is now three-dimensional! Just take it slowly and re-check your measurements as you go. At the top and bottom of the pocket you'll have the lines of sewing done in step 2 to guide you.) Set your front panel aside for now.

9   Lay your back piece out right side up in a portrait position. Measure 4.5cm (1¾in) down from the centre of the top edge and mark a point. Cut two strips of webbing each 13cm (5⅛in) long. Pin one of your strips of webbing across the back, so its centre matches up with the point you marked. Fold each end under by 1cm (⅜in) and pin. Fold your second piece of webbing into a loop, poke the cut ends under the first strip of webbing, at the centre, and pin in place.

10 Cut two 10cm (4in) lengths of webbing and thread each through a D-ring, bringing the ends together (see Sliders and D-rings on page 123 for more information). Place the webbing loops on top of the back piece, one 4cm (1½in) in from the left side and one the same distance in from the right, with the cut ends aligned with the bottom edge. Pin and then sew in place, 5mm (¼in) up from the bottom edge.

11 Cut two 80cm (31½in) lengths of webbing for the main straps. Tuck one end of each strap under the top of the strip pinned at the top of your panel, on either side of the loop. Pin in place.

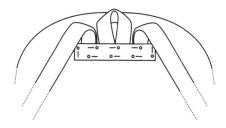

12 Thread the other end of one strap through the top of a strap adjuster from back to front, over the central bar and through to the back again, down and through the corresponding D-ring from front to back, then back up and over the central bar of the adjuster again as before – see Sliders and D-rings on page 123 for more information. With about 6.5cm (2½in) of webbing coming out of the adjuster, fold the end under by 1cm (⅜in) and pin to the strap at the back to make a loop. Repeat this step for the second strap.

13 Sew the two loops closed with two rows of stitching (I also added a few stitches by hand at the sides to stop any frayed ends showing).

14 Now sew all the way around the edge of the little strip that's holding your top loop and strap ends in place, about 2mm (⅟₁₆in) in from the edge. Sew twice to make sure it's secure. Set your back piece aside for now.

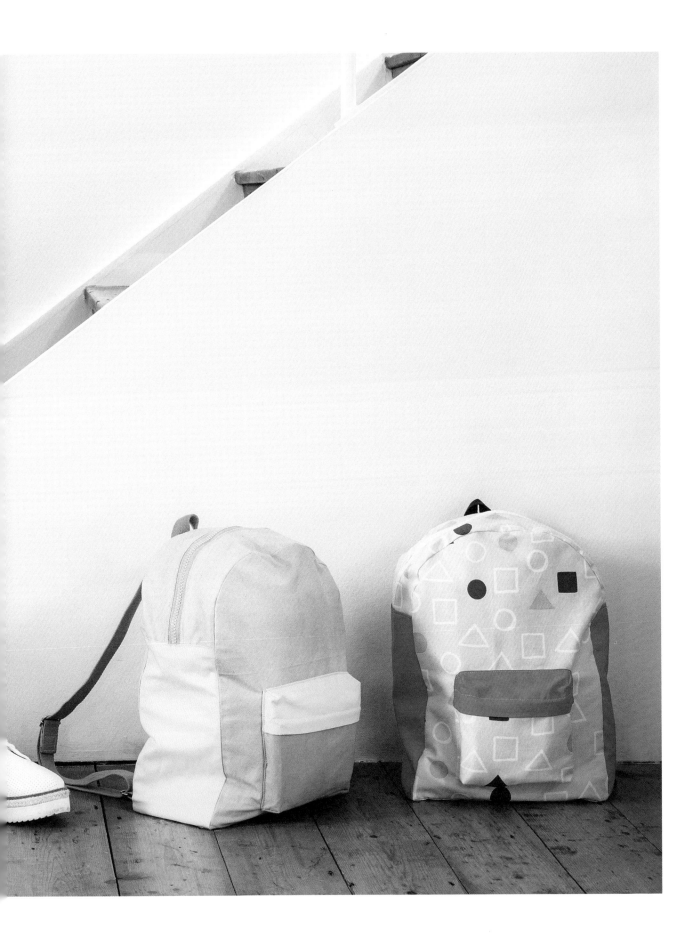

15 Lay out the side pieces in your main fabric right side up and lay one of the side pieces in your accent fabric on top of each, also right side up, and pin. You'll now treat the two layers as one, so turn both short edges under together by 1cm (⅜in) at one end only of each side piece – with the accent fabric right side out – and press. Sew along about 3mm (⅛in) from the folded edge.

16 Take the two zip edge pieces and fold each in half, wrong sides together, so the long edges meet, then press. Pin them along either side of your zip, with the folded edge closest to the zip and leaving a gap between them of about 1.5cm (⅝in) over the zip teeth. Sew along both sides (using your machine's zipper foot) about 2mm (¹⁄₁₆in) from the folded edges. Check your zip panel is 14cm (5½in) wide in total – trim along the long edges if necessary.

17 Next, lay out your front panel, right side up, and pin your side pieces in place, right side down, with the folded edges at the top and aligning the bottom corners. Pin one edge of your zip panel centred along the curved top of your front panel and with right sides facing, making sure the short ends overlap your side pieces by around 2.5cm (1in) on both sides. Change back to a regular sewing foot and sew your zip and side panels in place with a 1cm (⅜in) seam allowance.

18 Working right side out, pin the folded edges of your side panels to the zip panel beneath and sew about 3mm (⅛in) from the folded edge.

19 With right sides together, pin your back panel in place all the way around your side and zip panels. Sew in place with a 1cm (⅜in) seam allowance. Unzip your zip! Pin the base piece in place, right sides facing, lining up with the bottom edges of your front/back and side pieces, and sew in place with a 1cm (⅜in) seam allowance. Leave the bag wrong side out.

20 To prepare your lining, start by folding one of the short edges on each of your side pieces over by 1cm (⅜in) and pressing. Next, lay one of your back/front pieces right side up and place your side pieces on top, right side down, with folded edges at the top and aligning the bottom corners. Pin and then sew along the outer edge of each side piece with a 1cm (⅜in) seam allowance.

21 With right sides together, pin your other front/back lining piece to the other edge of your side pieces, then sew along the outer edges as before. Pin your base piece in place, with right sides together, lining up with the bottom edges of your front/back and side pieces, and sew in place with a 1cm (⅜in) seam allowance.

22 Turn your lining right side out. Slip your outer bag into the lining and line up all the edges and corners. Fold over the top edges of your front/back lining by 1cm (⅜in) and pin along the seam between your zip panel and outer front/back pieces. Also pin along the top edges of your lining side panels.

23 Hand sew your lining in place where you have pinned, then turn your bag right side out through the zip.

DESIGN NOTE

There are loads of different kinds of zips to choose from, and you could use any style you like, but I feel a chunky plastic zip fits really well with the slightly retro feel here.

Overnight Bag

Roomy but with a slim profile, this bag is big enough for your overnight essentials without feeling bulky to carry or stash.

Skill level ●●○

Materials

1m (1⅛yd) patterned medium-weight canvas fabric

¾m (⅞yd) lightweight wadding (batting)

½m (⅝yd) plain medium-weight canvas or quilting cotton for the lining

2m (2¼yd) heavy-weight webbing, 3cm (1¼in) wide

50cm (20in) zip to match your fabric

4 sets of snap fasteners with fixing tool

You can get these in a kit, but if you don't want to buy a snap fastener tool you could just use sew-in snap fasteners or hook-and-loop tape instead.

Thread to match your fabric and webbing

Basic sewing kit

Cut out

MAIN FABRIC

Two pieces: 52cm (20½in) wide x 47cm (18½in) high

Two pieces: 25cm (10in) wide x 19cm (7½in) high for inner pocket

Four pieces: 25cm (10in) wide x 19cm (7½in) high for outer pockets

Four pieces: 19.5cm (7¾in) wide x 8cm (3⅛in) high for outer pocket flaps

Two pieces: 7cm (2¾in) x 7cm (2¾in) for covering the strap ends

Two pieces: 3cm (1¼in) x 6cm (2⅜in) for zip end tabs

LINING FABRIC

Two pieces: 52cm (20½in) wide x 47cm (18½in) high

WADDING (BATTING)

Two pieces: 52cm (20½in) wide x 47cm (18½in) high

WEBBING

Two pieces: 87cm (34¼in) long

FABRIC NOTE

I love geometric fabric prints! Often they work best though when you take a little extra care in the cutting out and try to keep things symmetrical.

1   Lay out one of your wadding (batting) pieces in a landscape position and place one of your main fabric pieces right side up and aligned on top. Take one of your pieces of webbing and pin in place through all layers of your fabric/wadding (batting) as shown in the diagram, so it's 14cm (5½in) in from each side and with the ends 18.5cm (7¼in) from the top edge. Mark the webbing with chalk 6cm (2⅜in) down from the top edge of the fabric.

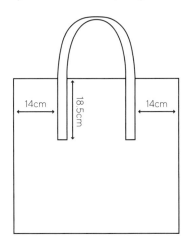

2   Starting at the cut end, sew along the webbing 2mm (¹⁄₁₆in) in from the outer edge – begin at one end, swivel at your mark to sew across the webbing, and back down the other side. Repeat this on the other handle end. Don't worry about the cut ends, as they'll be covered later!

3   Repeat steps 1 and 2 for your other main and wadding (batting) pieces and webbing. Set your outer pieces aside.

4   Next, make your inner pocket. Lay your two inner pocket pieces one on top of the other, with right sides facing and in a portrait position. Pin and then sew around the sides and bottom with a 1cm (⅜in) seam allowance. Turn right side out through the edge you left unsewn. Fold in the open edges by 1cm (⅜in), press with an iron and sew along 3mm (⅛in) in from the edge.

5   Lay out one of your lining pieces (right side up if it has a right side) in a landscape position and place your inner pocket 13cm (5⅛in) down from the top edge and an equal distance from both sides. Pin your pocket in place and sew along the side and bottom edges with a 3mm (⅛in) seam allowance. Set your lining piece aside.

6   Now we can make the outer pockets, so repeat step 4 with both pairs of outer pocket pieces.

7   Now take one pair of your pocket flap pieces and lay out right sides together in a landscape position. Pin and then sew around the sides and bottom with a 1cm (⅜in) seam allowance. Turn right side out through the edge you left unsewn. Fold in the unsewn edges by 1cm (⅜in) and press, but this time don't sew this edge up. Repeat with the other pair of flap pieces.

8   Following the instructions in the kit, add two positive snap halves to each of your pocket flaps (so the caps are on the outside) 4.5cm (1¾in) from the open edge and 5cm (2in) in from each side.

9   Take your outer pocket pieces (not the flap pieces) and concertina-fold the shorter edges in as shown in the diagram – folding twice, by 1.5cm (⅝in) each time. Iron well to hold the folds.

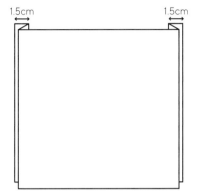

1.5cm   1.5cm

10 Lay out one of your main outer pieces, right side up, with the handle at the top. Place your outer pocket pieces as in the diagram – so they are 7cm (2¾in) in from the sides and 19.5cm (7¾in) down from the top edge. At the sides of your pockets, pin and sew 3mm (⅛in) in from the edge along the bottom layer only of the folded part. Then sew along the bottom, 3mm (⅛in) in from the edge.

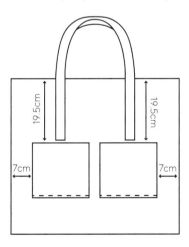

19.5cm   19.5cm

7cm   7cm

11 Place your pocket flap pieces (with the open edge at the top) 17.5cm (6⅞in) from the top edge of your main piece, so they overlap the top of your pockets by about 3.5cm (1⅜in). Their open edges should overlap the raw ends of your handle by 1cm (⅜in). Pin along the top of each flap and sew 2mm (1/16in) in from the edge, then 1.2cm (½in) in – this second row of stitching conceals the ends of the handle.

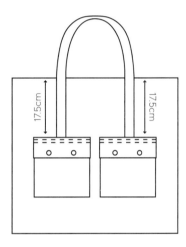

17.5cm   17.5cm

12 Mark the front of each of your pocket pieces, 5cm (2in) in from each side (check this lines up with the snaps on your pocket flaps and adjust slightly if necessary) and 1.5cm (⅝in) from the top edge of the pocket. Add two negative snap halves on each pocket, so the cap is on the inside. You should be able to close the pockets now with the snaps.

13 Lay the other main outer piece right side up, with the handle at the top. Take the two pieces of main fabric you cut for covering the strap ends and lay out right side down. Fold each edge over by 1cm (⅜in) to the wrong side and press. Turn your little squares over and pin them on top of the raw ends of your webbing. Sew around 3mm (⅛in) in from the edges.

14 Now you're ready to put your bag together! Start by preparing your zip. Place the two 3cm (1¼in) x 6cm (2⅜in) zip end tab pieces right side down and fold over both short edges of both pieces, pressing in place. Now fold each piece in half (right side out) so that the shorter folded ends meet. Place one tab over each end of your zip, so the zip tapes are sandwiched between the folded layers, and pin in place. Sew across about 3mm (⅛in) from the edge of your tabs.

15 Lay out the lining piece with the pocket side facing up, in a landscape position (make sure the pocket is also the right way up, with the opening at the top). Lay your zip right side up on top, so it lines up with the top long edge of your lining piece – see Inserting Zips on pages 126–127 for more information. Place your main outer piece without pockets on top, right side down with all edges aligned, and pin along the top edge (through the outer, zip and lining layers).

16 Change your sewing machine foot to a zipper foot. Sew along the top edge about 3mm (⅛in) from where you can feel the zip's teeth.

17 Unfold your outer and lining layers and fold back the other way, so that they are wrong sides together and you can see the zip.

18 Lay out your other lining piece (right side up if it has a right side) and lay the zip (with fabric now attached) on top, right side up, so its other edge lines up with the top edge of your lining, in the same way as before. Place the other main outer piece (with pockets) on top, right side down, lining up with the top edge. Pin in place and sew along that edge as before.

19 Fold back your fabric as in step 17 and iron along both sides of your zip, where the fabric seam is (be careful not to melt the zip). Pin along both sides, through the outer, zip and lining.

20 Change your machine foot back to an ordinary sewing foot, then sew where you have pinned, about 2mm (¹⁄₁₆in) from the seam between zip and fabric.

21 Unfold your fabric pieces again and refold so that the two lining pieces are right sides together and the two main pieces are right sides together with your zip pointing towards the lining.

22 Unzip your zip – this is easy to forget, but a really important step!

23 Pin all the way around, then sew 1cm (⅜in) in from the edges, leaving a 6cm (2⅜in) gap on one of the lining sides.

24 Square off each corner by flattening so the side seam is above the bottom seam and sewing a line across 4cm (1½in) from the corner of the seam – see Squaring Corners on pages 124–125 for more information.

25 Turn your bag right side out through the gap you left in the lining, and then sew up the gap (you can do this by machine or hand as it will be hidden inside the bag).

26 Tuck your lining down into your outer through the open zip.

DESIGN NOTE
To keep things extra organized you could add pockets to both sides rather than just one, and even add extra pockets inside!

Core Techniques

Making bias binding (tape)

Store-bought bias binding (tape) works just fine for the projects here that feature binding – but if you want to make them extra special try making your own, which gives you the freedom to create binding in exactly the colour or pattern you want. These instructions are based on making 2.5cm (1in) wide bias binding – your strips need to be about 2mm (1⁄16in) less than twice your final binding width, so you can use this to calculate for other widths of binding.

1   Start by cutting your strips of fabric. Lay out your chosen fabric right side down (you can use as little as a fat quarter, depending how much binding you need to make). Using your setsquare, draw a diagonal line across the fabric at 45 degrees to the fabric weave (i.e. 45 degrees to its straight edge). Draw more lines, each 4.8cm (1⅞in) from the last, on either side of your first line. Cut along your lines to create strips (a rotary cutter and cutting board are great for this).

2   To make your separate strips into one long strip, start by cutting across the angled end of your strips so they are now straight across. Lay one strip out right side up then lay a second right side down at a right angle to the first, so they overlap at one end as in the image.

3   Pin and then sew at a 45-degree angle across the corner, as shown. Unfold and press.

4   Continue adding more strips until you have the length you need.

5   Now we'll turn the strip(s) into binding. Feed a strip through the binding making tool (they usually come with a pointy tool to help you pull the first bit of fabric through), pressing it with a hot iron as you pull it through to crease the edges. And you're all done!

Drawstrings

Here's how to get neat edges at the openings of your drawstring channels.

1   At each of the top corners of your fabric, fold a narrow triangle in from the side (see specific projects for measurements), and then fold over again by the same amount and pin. Sew along the inner edges of both of your little triangles.

2   Here you can see images of how to thread a single or double drawstring. Use a safety pin at one end of your cord to help guide it through and one pinned across the other end to make sure it stays outside!

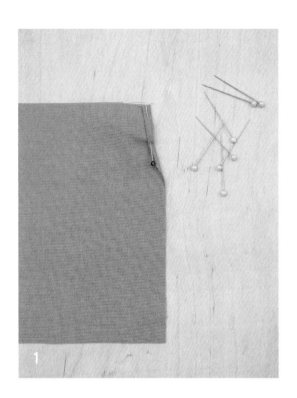

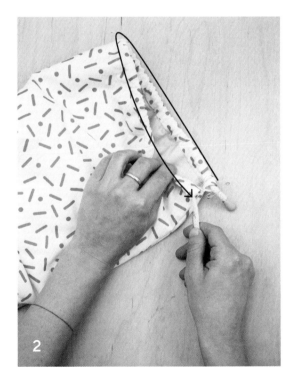

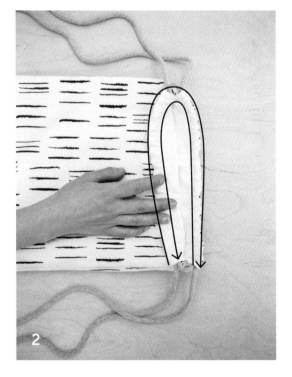

Interfacing, wadding and bag bottoms

I've used a few different interfacings and wadding (batting) for the projects collected here, and one bag even has a plastic bag bottom to add extra structure. These are all different ways to add structure or support to your fabrics.

I'm not big on rules, but as a guide, I use stiff fusible interfacing when I want structure without bulk – it's useful for things like clutch bags. Always follow the manufacturer's instructions when fusing the interfacing in place. Wadding (batting) gives a soft padded feel (but adds a little bulk), so I've used that for the iPad cases, whereas foam interfacing, which I've used for the Hand-luggage Bag, gives firmer, more structured padding, but adds a fair bit of bulk. Finally, I chose to add a bag bottom (a plastic grid insert that can be cut to size) in the hand-luggage bag so it holds its shape even when full.

When using stiff interfacing I usually go for fusible, which means you can iron it onto your fabric. It's always best to check the instructions on the particular brand of interfacing that you buy, but usually the aim is to 'press' rather than 'iron' and often a damp pressing cloth (a clean tea towel or similar) helps.

Piping

Piping can add a really finished look, or a pop of contrast, to a project. Here's how your piping should look as you sew it in place.

Sliders and D-rings

Here's how your sliders and D-rings should look for your backpack straps.

Squaring corners

A really simple way to add depth to a bag is to square off the corners.

1   Once you've sewn your seams, trim across the bottom corners, close to your stitching.

2   Flatten a corner as shown (the side seam should now run directly over the bottom edge's seam). Mark across the corner at a right angle to the side seam (the measurements to use will be given in the project – measure from the corner of the seam).

3   Sew along the line and finally trim the corner to avoid bulk.

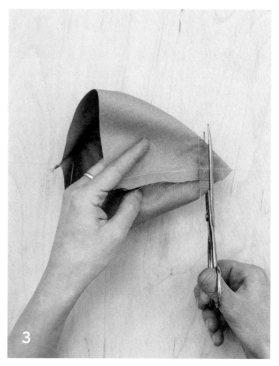

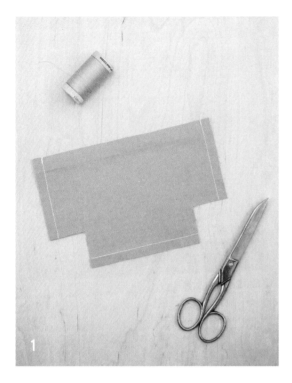

The Interview bag and Retro Backpack use a different technique for squaring the corners. I usually use the technique pictured on page 124, but in these projects this alternative method was more suitable.

1   Cut away a square at each bottom corner (see project for exact measurements).

2   Then bring the seams together.

3   Pin and sew along the edge.

Inserting zips

Here you can follow step-by-step pictures for how to add your zip (unlined projects will work a little differently).

1   Lay out a lining piece right side up and lay the zip on top, right side up, with its edge along the top edge of the lining.

2   Place the main fabric piece on top, right side down. Pin along the top edge about 3mm (⅛in) from the zip teeth and sew using a zipper foot on your machine.

3   After sewing, fold your pieces of fabric back so they are wrong sides together and you can see the zip again.

4   Lay out the other lining piece right side up and place the zip as before, along top edge and right side up. Place the other main piece right side down on top. Pin and sew as before.

5   Fold the fabric pieces back as before and press.

6   Change the zipper foot back to an ordinary foot. Pin and then sew along the fabric on either side of the zip, about 2mm (¹⁄₁₆in) from the seam.

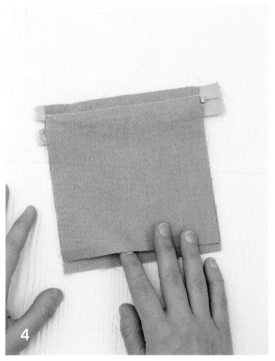

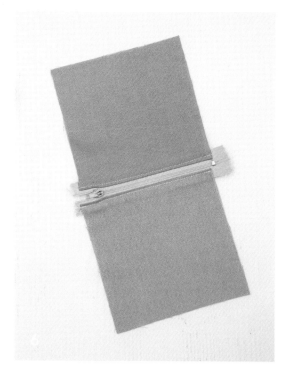

Zip tabs

Some of the projects call for tabs at the ends of your zips – these are small folded pieces of fabric, added before you fit your zip, that cover the zip tape ends and give an extra-neat, finished look.

Securing straps/ handles

Straps and handles can end up carrying a lot of weight, so sewing a square at each end with a central cross can be a great way to attach them securely.

Webbing straps/ handles

Webbing is great as a ready-made strip of handle/strap! Look out for different thicknesses of webbing as well as different widths. Personally I prefer the look and feel of cotton webbing rather than the artificial fibre alternatives.

You might also want to strengthen the part that you'll be holding, and also make it more comfortable when carrying heavier weights.

1   Fold the webbing in half along a central section and pin.

2   Then sew along the open edge, as shown here.

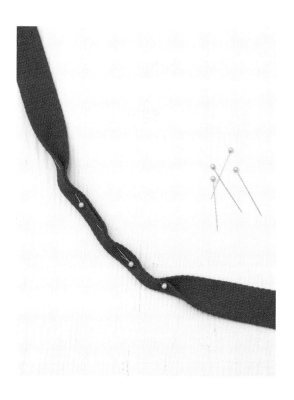

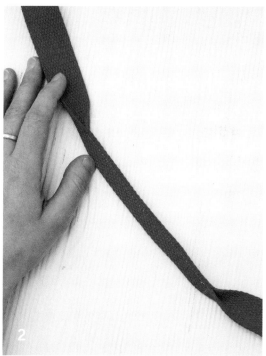

Curved edges

When we turn curved edges right way out they can bunch up if we don't cut some little snips into the seam to give it more movement. You want to cut close to the seam, but not too close!

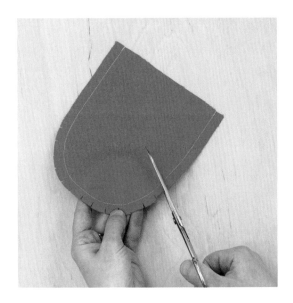

Making fabric straps/ handles

Here's how your strap/handle strips should look as they go from being strips of fabric to sturdy straps/handles. Your strips should start off four times the final width you are aiming for.

1   Fold a handle strip in half so the two long edges are together and press.

2   Unfold and then fold the long edges in to meet at the central crease, pressing again.

3   Finally, re-fold along the middle so the long raw edges are now concealed inside, and press again. Pin along the open edge.

4   Sew about 2mm (⅛in) in along both long edges of the folded strip.

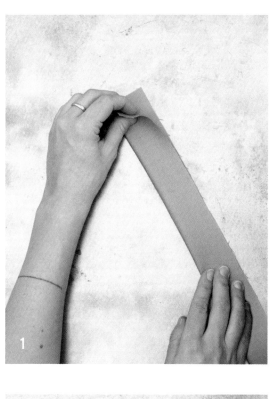

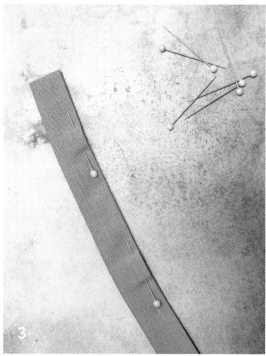

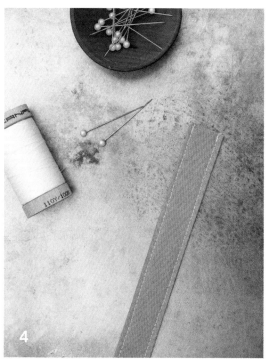

CIRCLE SHOULDER BAG A

POMPOM BUCKET BAG

CIRCLE SHOULDER BAG B

Templates

All the templates shown here are full-size (and
include seam allowance when relevant) so simply
trace, photocopy or scan them then cut them
out! If scanning, just double check your settings
and make sure they print to actual size. See inside
the back cover for the Contrast Clutch and Retro
Backpack templates.

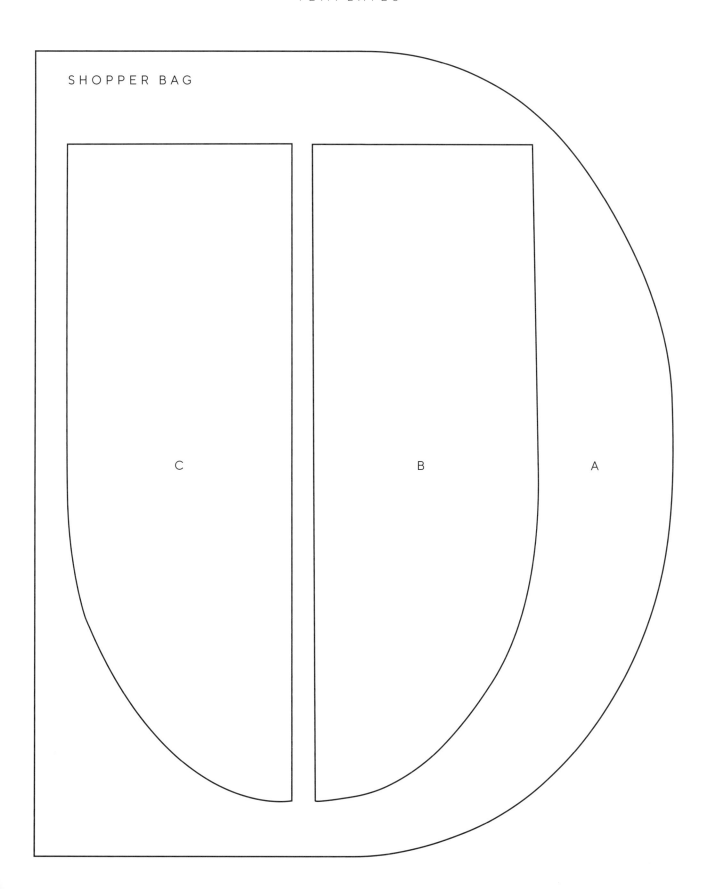

SHOPPER BAG

C

B

A

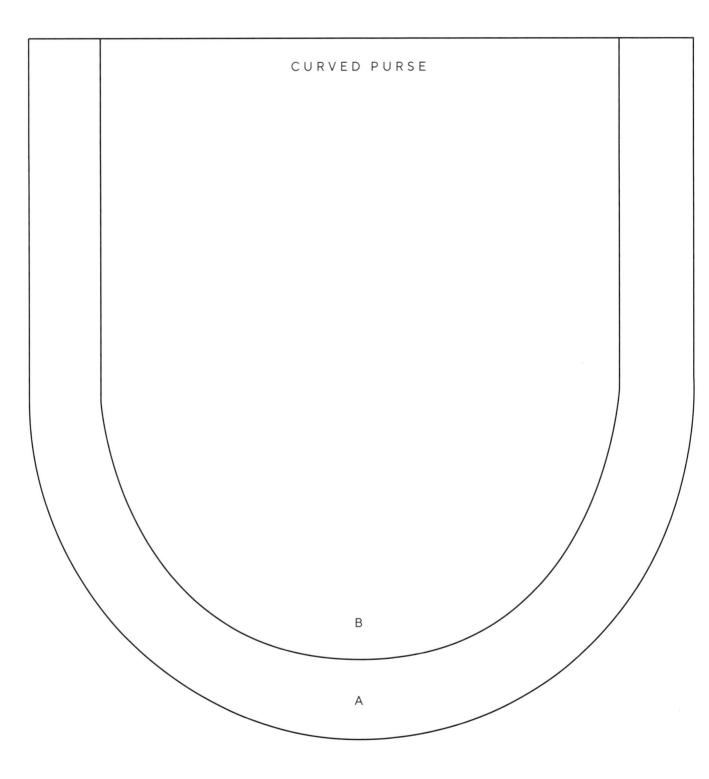

CURVED PURSE

B

A

Choosing the right fabrics

Choosing the fabric/s is one of my absolute favourite parts of making any bag! I've tried to give a bit of detail throughout this book about which kind of fabric works best for each project, for instance some projects need lighter fabrics like quilting-weight cotton (basically your standard light cotton fabric) and others need a bit of body like a medium- or heavy-weight canvas. Beyond those guidelines though, there's a huge amount of room to put your creative stamp on a project with your choice of fabric.

Many of the projects here work beautifully in plain solid colour fabrics but you can still make these your own by thinking about the relationship between the main colour and the details – do you want a neutral, timeless look with details subtly complementing the main fabric colour, or a bold statement with sharp contrasts? I tend to start with the main fabric and then play about with laying webbing or zips on top to see how they might work together.

Patterned fabrics are especially fun to choose as you get to look through so many beautiful designs (check out my list of favourite fabric brands on page 137)! There's also so much room for your own style here. Things to think about when choosing patterned fabrics include scale (will the pattern be too chunky or too detailed for a particular project), and once again the relationship to details like zips or handles. It can work really well to pick out a colour from your patterned fabric for the details so all the elements feel more unified.

There's not just the main, outer fabric to think about, as most of the projects also have a lining fabric. Whilst the lining can be just a practical element, making your bag look finished and adding some extra structure, it can also be a design statement! I love to use a patterned fabric to line a plain bag (like in the Interview Bag), adding some subtle personality. Similarly a contrasting colour can add a pop of interest to a simple bag. If using a light coloured outer fabric though, just check your lining fabric won't show through!

If you're quite new to choosing fabrics it's a good idea to spend some time in a haberdashery shop to get a sense of the textures and weights of different types of fabric. Getting a feel for what descriptions such as 'medium-weight canvas' or 'cotton twill' mean makes it much easier to shop online (though if in doubt, you can often order samples).

Finally, don't be afraid to go a bit off-piste to find the right fabric! The pompom bucket bag is the perfect example of this – I couldn't find a heavy enough fabric with the kind of pattern I was looking for, but I found a cotton rug that was perfect, so I used that!! Of course there can be challenges to cutting up rugs (or old clothes, or tablecloths, or curtains...) to use as fabric, but sometimes half the fun is experimenting!

Finding your style and how to design your own bags

There's so much room for exploring your own style through the projects in this book, and maybe even using them as a springboard to designing your own bags! Nothing is set in stone here, so always feel free to change things about, whether it's a different colour scheme, longer straps, more pockets, different closures... Whatever works for you!

Some of the simpler projects like the Curved Purse and the Basic Tote offer a great way to experiment with different fabrics, zips and straps quickly and easily, so why not try out a few versions of each to get a feel for your style. These simple projects are also a good place to start experimenting with adding your own details. The core techniques pages can be really useful here – you could try adding piping to a different project or swapping out webbing for hand-made fabric straps.

When I design a bag I try to think about two aspects in equal measure – how it will be useful and how I can make it look good! Often the practicalities actually inspire the aesthetics. Designing the Oversized Beach Bag, for instance, I was thinking about how to make it really roomy, easy to chuck stuff in and comfortable to carry. Giving it a lot of depth to make it roomy got me thinking about making a feature of the sides using contrasting fabric and I decided to use the same contrasting fabric for comfy fabric handles too! This is a great way to start designing your own bags, making sure they're perfect for their purpose and gorgeous too!

Suppliers

UK FABRIC

I love these independent UK online fabric suppliers (who also ship internationally):

The Fabric Fox
thefabricfox.co.uk

M is for Make
misformake.co.uk

Ray Stitch
raystitch.co.uk

The Crafty Mastermind
thecraftymastermind.co.uk

The Draper's Daughter
drapersdaughter.com

For ethically produced fabrics I also love:

Offset Warehouse
offsetwarehouse.com

Organic Textile Company
organiccotton.biz

And for handles, straps and other bag hardware check out:

U-handbag
u-handbag.com

WORLDWIDE FABRIC

Anna Ka Bazaar (Europe)
annakabazaar.com

Fibresmith (Australia)
fibresmith.com.au

Miss Matatabi Japanese Fabric (Japan)
shop.missmatatabi.com

Purl Soho (USA)
purlsoho.com

Simplifi Fabric (Canada)
simplififabric.com

Stoff & Stil (Europe)
stoffstil.com

The Drapery (Australia)
thedrapery.com.au

Threadbare Fabrics (USA)
threadbarefabrics.com

FABRIC BRANDS

These are some of the fabric brands I particularly love. Most are stocked worldwide online.

Atelier Brunette
atelierbrunette.com

Cloud9 Fabrics
cloud9fabrics.com

Cotton + Steel
cottonandsteelfabrics.com

Dashwood Studio
dashwoodstudio.com

Kona Solids by Robert Kaufman
(really handy range of solid colour quilting-weight cotton fabric)
robertkaufman.com

Index

Acknowledgements

Huge thanks to Harriet Butt for believing in the idea (and sticking with it!), Emily Lapworth for the beautiful design work, and both for being completely wonderful to work with. Thank you Anna Batchelor and Tam Dhondy for the beautiful photography and styling, and for lovely shoot-day chats! Thank you Harriet Webster and Saumya Mittal for your modelling skills and to the rest of the team behind the scenes at Quadrille.

Thank you to all the wonderful fabric designers and independent fabric shops whose work makes my job so much easier! Thank you to everyone in the making community for being such a kind and generous bunch!

Thank you to my loved ones for all your support and enthusiasm, and especially to Calder for sometimes letting me get almost enough sleep.

About the author

Anna Alicia is a designer–maker, freelance craft writer for magazines including *Mollie Makes* and *Simply Sewing*, and a mother. She lives in East London with her artist/academic partner and their little boy. When Anna isn't sewing, she can mostly be found roaming the parks of East London with the little one.

Anna's aim is always to keep things simple and she hopes this results in her projects being accessible, enjoyable and affordable for makers of all levels. Anna's first book *Make it Your Own* focused on interior makes (which seems improbable now that her home is mostly covered in Duplo and crayons), but Anna hopes to continue its ethos of encouraging readers to use her projects as a springboard to explore their own creativity through this new book.

PUBLISHING DIRECTOR
Sarah Lavelle

COMMISSIONING EDITOR
Harriet Butt

DESIGN AND ART DIRECTION
Emily Lapworth

PHOTOGRAPHER
Anna Batchelor

PROP STYLIST
Tamineh Dhondy

PRODUCTION DIRECTOR
Vincent Smith

PRODUCTION CONTROLLER
Katie Jarvis

Published in 2019 by Quadrille,
an imprint of Hardie Grant Publishing

Quadrille
52–54 Southwark Street
London SE1 1UN
quadrille.com

Cataloguing in Publication Data:
a catalogue record for this book is
available from the British Library.

ISBN 978 1 78713 376 1
Printed in China